Holthausen, Richard; Czaplewski, Raymond L.; DeLorenzo, Don; Hayward, Greg; Kessler, Winifred B.; Manley, Pat; McKelvey, Kevin S.; Powell, Douglas S.; Ruggiero, Leonard F.; Schwartz, Michael K.; Van Horne, Bea; Vojta, Christina D. 2005. **Strategies for monitoring terrestrial animals and habitats**. Gen. Tech. Rep. RMRS-GTR-161. Fort Collins, CO: U.S. Department of Agriculture, Forest Service, Rocky Mountain Research Station. 34 p.

Abstract

This General Technical Report (GTR) addresses monitoring strategies for terrestrial animals and habitats. It focuses on monitoring associated with National Forest Management Act planning and is intended to apply primarily to monitoring efforts that are broader than individual National Forests. Primary topics covered in the GTR are monitoring requirements; ongoing monitoring programs; key monitoring questions and measures; balancing three necessary and complementary forms of monitoring (targeted, cause-and-effect, and context); sampling design and statistical considerations; use of the data that result from monitoring; and organizational and operational considerations in the development and implementation of monitoring programs. The GTR concludes with a series of recommendations for the ongoing improvement of monitoring of terrestrial animals and their habitat.

The Authors

Richard Holthausen: Washington Office, Watershed, Fish and Wildlife, Flagstaff, AZ

Raymond L. Czaplewski: Rocky Mountain Research Station, Fort Collins, CO

Don DeLorenzo: Southwestern Region, Albuquerque, NM

Greg Hayward: Rocky Mountain Region, Denver, CO

Winifred B. Kessler: Alaska Region, Juneau, AK

Pat Manley: Pacific Southwest Research Station, Sierra Nevada Research Center, Davis, CA

Kevin S. McKelvey: Rocky Mountain Research Station, Missoula, MT

Douglas S. Powell: Washington Office, Ecosystem Management Coordination, Washington, DC

Leonard F. Ruggiero: Rocky Mountain Research Station, Missoula, MT

Michael K. Schwartz: Rocky Mountain Research Station, Missoula, MT

Bea Van Horne: Washington Office, Wildlife, Fish, Water, and Air Research, Washington, DC

Christina D. Vojta: Washington Office, Watershed, Fish and Wildlife, Flagstaff, AZ

You may order additional copies of this publication by sending your mailing information in label form through one of the following media. Please specify the publication title and number.

Telephone	(970) 498-1392
FAX	(970) 498-1396
E-mail	rschneider@fs.fed.us
Web site	http://www.fs.fed.us/rm
Mailing Address	Publications Distribution Rocky Mountain Research Station 240 West Prospect Road Fort Collins, CO 80526

Strategies for Monitoring Terrestrial Animals and Habitats

Richard Holthausen, Raymond L. Czaplewski, Don DeLorenzo, Greg Hayward, Winifred B. Kessler, Pat Manley, Kevin S. McKelvey, Douglas S. Powell, Leonard F. Ruggiero, Michael K. Schwartz, Bea Van Horne, Christina D. Vojta

Contents

Preface

The original version of this report was prepared at the request of Forest Service Regional Directors of wildlife who wanted a team to provide recommendations for monitoring terrestrial animals and species on National Forests and Grasslands. This General Technical Report (GTR) was developed from that internal report. It focuses on monitoring associated with National Forest Management Act planning and is intended to apply primarily to monitoring efforts whose scope is broader than individual National Forests. Much of the GTR focuses on the Forest Service's organization and programs. However, the concepts described for making critical choices in monitoring programs and efficiently combining different forms of monitoring should be broadly applicable within other organizations.

EXECUTIVE SUMMARY

Monitoring of terrestrial animals and their habitats on National Forests and Grasslands is motivated largely by the National Forest Management Act (NFMA) and regulations implementing the act. Regulations that were issued in 1982 required monitoring of Management Indicator Species (MIS) and their habitats, determination of the relationship between populations and habitat, and determination of the effects of management. New regulations published in 2005 contain only a general requirement for monitoring indicators of ecological sustainability but do not contain specific wildlife monitoring requirements. The increased flexibility in the new regulations will not necessarily eliminate monitoring of animal populations, but they should allow us to reconsider the question of what monitoring information will be most useful to inform needed adjustments to management plans over both the short and long term.

Monitoring for terrestrial animals on National Forests and Grasslands has been problematic. At the level of individual Forests and Grasslands, monitoring efforts are frequently marked by inadequate design and insufficient funds to reliably detect trends. Terrestrial animal monitoring efforts that address multiple Forests tend to be better designed and funded. However, these tend to be focused on Federally listed or otherwise highly visible species, and just three of these efforts account for nearly $4 million in annual budget.

In order for monitoring to be useful in adaptive management, monitoring must be able to distinguish the effects of local activities (e.g., management of a single National Forest) from broad-scale effects such as those that might result from disease or climatic patterns. It must also provide information on causes of trends. Without such information, managers will not be able to properly interpret trends or know what actions to take to alter unfavorable trends. With those considerations in mind, we suggest that monitoring programs for terrestrial animals and their habitats be designed to answer the following five questions:

1. Are species, habitat, and community objectives being achieved consistent with outcomes anticipated in Forest plans?

2. Are species, habitats, and communities responding to specific management activities and the effects of those activities as anticipated in Forest plans?

3. What are the status and trends of species, habitats, and communities of concern and interest for which there are not specific anticipated outcomes in Forest plans (e.g., invasives, some sensitive species, species or groups of special interest)?

4. What are the status and trends of broader measures of biological diversity and ecosystem change for which there are not specific anticipated outcomes in Forest plans?

5. What are the mechanisms underlying change in habitats and communities, and species responses to changes in ecological conditions?

Questions 1, 2, 3, and 5 focus on species, habitats and communities that are considered of concern or interest in Forest plans. However, in most cases it will not be possible to monitor all such species. We suggest criteria to narrow the list of species to be monitored, but even after application of the criteria there are likely to be too many candidates for monitoring. Further prioritization may be accomplished by using ecological modeling and by focusing on legal obligations and species at highest risk.

In order to respond to the monitoring questions, three separate types of monitoring are needed:

- Targeted—monitors the condition and response to management of species and habitats that are identified as being of concern or interest
- Cause-and-effect—investigates the mechanisms that underlie habitat and species response to management and other forms of disturbance
- Context—monitors a broad array of ecosystem components at multiple scales without specific reference to influences of ongoing management

Creating balanced programs incorporating all three types of monitoring within realistic budgets will be a significant challenge. We suggest that this balancing be done at the Regional or higher level rather than at the scale of individual Forests so that appropriate consideration is given to monitoring that must be conducted across broad spatial extents. Assigning priorities at the Regional or higher scale should also result in greater consideration of the need for context and cause-and-effect monitoring. Appropriate balance among the three types of monitoring will be influenced by the state of knowledge of species and their habitats within an area, and the levels of risk to those species and habitats.

All monitoring must be designed to comply with the Data Quality Act. Monitoring programs must use best available science; employ sound statistical methods with effect size and power appropriate to the objective; identify sources of error; provide for quality assurance in data collection; and be subjected to peer review.

Modification of some facets of the current Forest Service organizational structure could be considered in order to improve effectiveness of our monitoring programs. We suggest that the Regions be given a larger role in the coordination of monitoring of terrestrial animals, and that such coordination would require some new dedicated positions. We also suggest that new funding mechanisms are needed to provide a reliable source of funds for multi-Forest efforts. Monitoring should be a collaborative effort between National Forest Systems (NFS) and Research and Development (R&D),

requiring a careful definition of roles and innovative, collaborative relationships. Partnerships and inter-agency coordination should play a much larger role in the future in monitoring of terrestrial animals and their habitats.

The report concludes with the following recommendations:

Make a national commitment to improve monitoring of terrestrial animals and their habitats.

Ensure that all monitoring contributes to adaptive management by exploring both the causes for trends and alternative scenarios that could reverse unfavorable trends.

Ensure that all monitoring complies with USDA Data Quality Guidelines.

Implement Regional monitoring strategies that integrate habitat and population monitoring. Monitoring habitat alone will rarely be sufficient for adaptive management because habitat relationships are not well understood and may not be predictable.

Adopt and integrate three types of monitoring (context, targeted, and cause-and-effect).

Use sound ecological principles and risk assessment to prioritize and design monitoring activities.

Recognize that monitoring is multi-scalar. Coordinate across ecological and administrative scales, with emphasis on the role of the Regions.

Establish appropriate roles and coordination for NFS and R&D from the Washington Office through Forest levels.

Provide adequate staffing, skills, and funding structures to accomplish monitoring objectives.

Use partnerships and interagency coordination to accomplish monitoring objectives.

Ensure that individuals and teams responsible for monitoring, development, and oversight have appropriate skills.

Chapter 1

Background

Monitoring Under the National Forest Management Act

The issue of wildlife monitoring on National Forest System (NFS) lands has been problematic for decades, at least since the development of regulations (Federal Register, 1982, Vol. 47, No. 190, 43037-43052) for the National Forest Management Act (NFMA) in 1982. Those regulations required monitoring at the scale of the plan area (generally a single National Forest or Grassland), focused monitoring on a set of Management Indicator Species (MIS)[1], and required that changes in population be related to changes in habitats. The 1982 regulations sparked ongoing debates over the choice of MIS, the appropriate scale for monitoring, the utility of population monitoring, the need for statistical reliability in data, responsibilities of the Forest Service and other agencies, and the ability to relate population changes to habitat changes resulting from management. Monitoring was frequently the target of both legal challenges and scientific criticisms.

New NFMA regulations published in 2005 (Federal Register, 2005, Vol. 70, No. 3, 1055-1061) require monitoring of indicators of ecological sustainability. While terrestrial animals and their habitats may be included within the set of indicators chosen by a Forest, the regulations do not contain specific wildlife monitoring requirements. These regulations also require that National Forests and Grasslands establish Environmental Management Systems (EMS), which are a set of processes and practices that enable an organization to track and manage its environmental impacts[2]. EMS will require monitoring, but the form of that monitoring is not clear. During the transition from the old to the new regulations, National Forests that continue to operate under the 1982 regulations will be allowed to satisfy MIS monitoring requirements through consideration of habitat and not populations.

While the requirements in the NFMA regulation are a key consideration in the development of monitoring plans, it is impossible to second guess what these requirements will be in the future. So, while the requirements deserve consideration, we also need to ask a much more fundamental question: what monitoring information will allow us to make needed adjustments to management plans over both the short term and long term? Focus on this question will be more valuable over the long term than trying to second guess future changes in regulations.

Current Wildlife and Habitat Monitoring

Overview of existing monitoring activities and programs for terrestrial species

On Forest Service System lands, approximately 700 species of terrestrial vertebrates and 500 invertebrates have one or more designations as federally listed, regionally sensitive, or Forest management indicator species, but only around 30 species are monitored with consistently funded monitoring programs, either at the multi-Forest level (table 1) or at the level of the individual national Forest or grassland (table 2). Of these, only 14 monitoring programs are funded by NFS at $100,000 or greater, while other programs operate on $30,000 to $80,000 annually. Funding of terrestrial animal species monitoring tends to be disproportionately allocated to a few high profile species. For example, the Forest Service contribution to the annual monitoring budget for northern spotted owls and red-cockaded woodpeckers is $1 to 1.5 million per year for each species, including administration, data analysis, and reports (table 1). The Forest Service contribution to grizzly bear monitoring is $250,000 annually through normal appropriations plus an additional $1.1 million Congressional earmark for FY04. These funds do not include the contributions of other monitoring partners, most of which are federal or state agencies.

In addition to monitoring programs for individual species, long-term avian monitoring programs exist in several Forest Service Regions (table 3). These multi-species bird monitoring programs, often called "landbird"

---

[1]MIS are defined in the 1982 regulations (36 CFR 219.19) as "species... selected because their population changes are believed to indicate the effects of management activities".

[2]http://www.iso-14001.org.uk/iso-14004.htm

USDA Forest Service Gen. Tech. Rep. RMRS-GTR-161. 2005

1

Table 1—Forest Service FY04 contributions to monitoring programs for terrestrial species at multi-forest or regional scales. Expenditures are approximate within 10% of the actual.

Species	Federal status	Regions involved	NFS FY04 contribution$
Northern Spotted Owl	T	5,6	1,620,000
Grizzly Bear, 1-yr Congressional earmk	T	1	1,100,000
Red-cockaded Woodpecker	E	8,9	1,000,000
Carnivores (Sierra Nevada)	C (fisher)	5	550,000
California Spotted Owl		5	450,000
Marbled Murrelet	T	6	400,000
Yosemite Toad and Yellow-legged Frog	Both C	5	314,000
Grizzly Bear (standard program)	T	1,2,4,6	250,000
Birds and Burns Network		1,2,4,6	234,000
Southwest Willow Flycatcher	E	3	150,000
Willow Flycatcher (California)		5	115,000
Mexican Spotted Owl	T	3	80,000
Chiricahua Leopard Frog	T	4	80,000
Pileated and white-headed woodpecker		4	60,000
Amphibian inventory (Montana)		1	50,000
Bats (Oregon bat grid)		6	40,000
Spotted Frog	C	4	36,000
Kirtland's Warbler	E	9	30,000
Canada Goose: Dusky and Vancouver		10	30,000
Black Swift		2, 3, 4,10	Not available
Boreal Toad	C	2,3,4	Not available
Black-tailed Prairie Dog	C	2	Not available

Table 2—Forest-level monitoring programs for terrestrial species where the NFS contribution is $50,000 or greater for FY04. Estimates are within 10% of the actual.

Species	Federal status	Region	Forest	FY04 contribution$
Multiple Species		1	Idaho Panhandle	500,000
Multiple Species (MSIM)		5	Tahoe	400,000
Northern Goshawk		3	Kaibab	300,000
Northern Goshawk		4	Dixie	60,000
Northern Goshawk		10	Tongass	75,000
Mexican Spotted Owl	T	3	Lincoln	250,000
Canada Lynx	T	9	Superior	125,000
Indiana Bat*	E	9	Monongahela	100,000
Chiricahua Leopard Frog	T	3	Coronado	80,000
Riparian birds		5	Tahoe	55,000
Northern Flying Squirrel	E	9	Monongahela	50,000

*Most forests with Indiana bat conduct project clearance work only.

monitoring, have been in place for two to 12 years, and annual costs, including administration, data analysis, and reports, are between $15,000 and $250,000.

Habitat monitoring—the FIA program

The Forest Inventory and Analysis (FIA) program is the nation's coast-to-coast forest inventory program and has been in continuous operation since 1930. FIA is primarily designed as a continuous forest census. Plots are permanently marked and revisited on a 10-year cycle.

FIA also has current and future potential for the inventory and monitoring of wildlife habitat, and it is therefore included here as an on going monitoring program. The FIA program is managed by Forest Service Research and Development (R&D) and when fully funded, the program costs $72 million annually.

The current FIA sample design consists of a systematic hexagonal grid across all ownerships in the United States, with each hexagon containing approximately 6000 ac (2360 ha). The inventory program consists of three

2

USDA Forest Service Gen. Tech. Rep. RMRS-GTR-161. 2005

Table 3—National Forest System landbird monitoring programs that are multi-Forest or regional in scope.

Program	Started	Annual cost
Fire and Fire Surrogates (bird monitoring portion)	2000	400,000
Birds and Burns	2002	234,000
Northern Region Landbird Monitoring Program	1994	200,000
Monitoring Colorado Birds	1998	200,000
Monitoring Wyoming Birds	2003	200,000
Southern Region Neotrop and Resident Landbirds	1996	250,000
Songbird Monitoring in the Great Lakes	1991	55,000
Late-successional Forest Birds in the Pacific NW	1994	15,000
Prairie bird monitoring	2001	35,000
Nevada Bird Count	2002	140,000
MAPS in Pacific Northwest Region	1994	70,000

phases. Phase 1 is a remote sensing phase aimed at classifying the land into forest and non-forest and obtaining spatial data such as fragmentation, urbanization, and distance variables. Phase 2 provides the bulk of information and consists of field data collected at one randomly located point within each hexagon. Vegetation structure and composition are measured at a cluster of plots associated with this sample point. At the present time, non-forest points are only sampled as necessary to quantify rates of land use change, and field measurements are not used to develop detailed information on non-forest vegetation. Phase 3 of data collection is conducted at a relatively small subset of the grid points (approximately 6%) and consists of an extended suite of ecological data including full forest-vegetation inventory, tree and crown condition, soil data, lichen diversity, measures of coarse woody debris, and ozone damage. From all three phases, FIA generates reports on the status and trends in forest conditions and makes the raw data available to NFS for site-specific analysis and interpretation. Many Regions rely on FIA points as training data for generating vegetation maps for Forest and project planning, and they also measure non-forest sites with FIA Phase 2 protocols to complete their vegetation databases. The FIA program is implemented in cooperation with a variety of partners including State forestry agencies and private landowners who grant access to non-federal lands for data collection purposes.

The utility of existing programs

Most of the current wildlife population monitoring programs are intended to produce simple trend data for individual species. The best examples of these programs are those directed at federally listed species. Under these programs, data are generally collected by multiple agencies and landowners and given directly to the Fish and Wildlife Service or to a university. The receiving agency or university takes responsibility for collating and analyzing the data across all ownerships within the range of the species, and then distributing reports. Forest Service units benefit from the reports by incorporating recent trends into project and Forest plans. Red-cockaded woodpecker monitoring is an example of such a program. Each National Forest has a budget for collecting data and the results are compiled by the Fish and Wildlife Service with those of other landowners across the range of the woodpecker.

The "landbird" (table 3) monitoring programs represent the only multiple-species monitoring for terrestrial vertebrates currently in place in NFS. Unfortunately each of these programs uses a different design, so it is difficult to aggregate or compare data between programs. Nevertheless, the data have proven valuable for the National Forests. In many cases, these regional programs provide the only capability for determining avian population trends for the National Forests. The Northern Rockies Landbird Monitoring Program has been underway for 12 years, and preliminary trends are available for approximately 60 species. The Songbird Monitoring in the Great Lakes program also has 12 years of data and has done trend analyses for 66 species. Both programs post trend information on the web, so that it is available for Forest planning and other applications. Other landbird programs are of shorter duration and have not yet evaluated trends. Due to methodological issues, the reliability of some generated trend data has been questioned (Ellingson and Lukacs 2003, Hutto and Young 2003).

FIA data have been used in numerous ways to provide broad scale context for assessing status and trends of wildlife habitat (Rudis 2004). Barnes (1979) gleaned information from FIA on foliage structure, browse/mast availability, and snag/wolf tree density to assess habitat

USDA Forest Service Gen. Tech. Rep. RMRS-GTR-161. 2005

3

of gray squirrels in Ohio and Pennsylvania. Brooks and others (1986) evaluated changes in white-tailed deer habitat in Maine from the 1950s to the 1980s, and similarly, Brooks (1990) evaluated raptor habitat changes for the same time period across the 11 northeastern states, using cover type, successional stage, and land ownership data from FIA. Flather and others (1989) used FIA along with a number of other broad scale information sources to create models predicting changes in white-tailed deer and turkey habitat in the southern United States. O'Brien (1990) conducted bird point counts at FIA points in Arizona and correlated bird numbers with FIA forest structure variables. Ohmann and others (1994) assessed the characteristics and density of snags for primary cavity-nesting birds using FIA data from nonfederal forest lands in Oregon and Washington. Chojnacky and Dick (2000) used FIA data to calculate stand density measures for assessing habitat of Mexican spotted owl in New Mexico.

The need for improvement to existing monitoring programs

Several patterns emerge from these ongoing, broadscale monitoring programs. They are strongly directed toward high-profile species, with the bulk of funds going to three federally listed species. Currently there are no population monitoring programs for any MIS that are as intensive as the monitoring efforts for federally listed or candidate species.

Taxonomically, these broad-scale monitoring programs focus primarily on birds (tables 1, 2, and 3). There is very little monitoring of mammals, except where these species are federally listed (grizzly bear, lynx) or candidates for listing (fisher). The Forest Service relies heavily on state agencies for data on game birds and mammals. There are few instances of amphibian monitoring, either for groups of species or for single species. There are no substantial monitoring programs for reptiles or invertebrates.

In addition to the broad-scale monitoring programs, there are examples of monitoring activities at the scale of individual National Forests. Some of these programs are well-designed, but most share common pitfalls. First, many of the individual Forest programs lack well-stated objectives. Frequently, the programs simply aim to verify that a species still occurs where it was found in previous years. This is sometimes called persistence monitoring, but the area or population of inference is unknown, and the resulting data are of limited use for informing management decisions.

Other pitfalls are a lack of sampling design and a lack of involvement of statisticians. Although many of these monitoring programs have an explicit protocol for data collection, the vast majority have no overall protocol for sample design. Plots are frequently placed in the best available habitat for a species, with no effort to randomize or to sample systematically. The sampling frame is not clearly specified, which makes it difficult or impossible to identify an area of inference. Many monitoring programs produce data that cannot be effectively evaluated because flawed statistical designs limit the ability to test hypotheses or quantify confidence limits.

Many Forest Service monitoring activities fail to involve Forest Service Research and Development (R&D) and therefore miss opportunities to gain enhanced knowledge about observed trends. Ideally, long-term trend monitoring could be associated with specific research projects that investigate possible explanations for observed trends.

Current wildlife and habitat monitoring programs need to be improved in order to provide high quality information for decisions made by land managers. Improvements are needed in monitoring design, coordination, and implementation. Based on our review of current Forest Service monitoring activities, the most successful monitoring programs have the following characteristics:

1. They have clearly stated objectives and a statistically sound sample design and have involved the research community and statisticians from their inception.

2. Monitoring is conducted in conjunction with related research studies to investigate potential causes of observed trends.

3. Successful monitoring programs effectively utilize partnerships for funding, political leverage, research expertise, and field assistance.

4. Data are collected under written protocol, by trained personnel, with established controls for data quality.

5. Costs of data management and analysis are included in the monitoring costs, with data management performed at frequent intervals and data analysis conducted at the end of each data collection period.

6. Data and results are made available through published reports or websites.

7. Programs encompass large geographic areas, which makes the results applicable at a scale that is meaningful for populations of species with broad ranges. Because of their broad geographic extent, these programs also attract more partners and therefore benefit from secure funding. There are many examples of successful small scale monitoring programs, but too often, small scale programs fail due to lack of consistent funds, inadequate statistical support, and inappropriate spatial extent for the monitoring question and species of interest.

Chapter 2

Questions and Measures

This chapter describes strategic planning of monitoring for terrestrial animal species and habitats. The process begins with identification of key monitoring questions to be addressed. Those questions help determine which biological elements (populations, species, communities, habitats) will be monitored. The monitoring questions, combined with logistical considerations, also drive the selection of specific measures (presence/absence, abundance, etc.) that will be monitored for each of the elements.

Monitoring Questions

The general goal and requirement for conservation of species and ecosystems on National Forests and Grasslands is provided in the NFMA, which directs Forest and Grassland units to "provide for diversity of plant and animal communities based on the suitability and capability of the specific land area in order to meet overall multiple-use objectives." The NFMA regulations, Forest Service directive system, and regulations implementing the Endangered Species Act (ESA) provide additional guidance for achieving this general goal. The objectives for monitoring should reflect both the general goal of providing diversity and the specific requirements for species contained in regulations and directives. Based on these requirements, the National Center for Ecological Analysis and Synthesis articulated three general objectives for monitoring of terrestrial animals in the National Forests and Grasslands (Andelman and others 2001). These are to:

- Improve our knowledge of the effects of ongoing management activities on species and the ecological conditions that support them. There are two components to this objective. The first is to determine the effect of individual management actions on species and their habitats, and the second is to determine the cumulative effect of combined management actions and natural processes under a given plan on species and habitats. As a practical matter, this objective is likely to be focused on particular species identified to be of interest or concern.
- Provide a more complete understanding of species and system dynamics in order to facilitate adaptive

management. Understanding the effects of ongoing management is an important part of a monitoring program but will not in itself provide the information needed to effectively modify management. To effectively modify management, we require information on the mechanisms underlying management effects on species and habitats.

- Improve our knowledge of the status of a broad array of species and the ecological conditions that support them. Status of species is affected by many factors in addition to Forest Service management and conditions on National Forests and Grasslands. Information on the status of a broad array of species provides better understanding of the influences of National Forest System lands and other ownerships on species, overall diversity, and which species should be considered of concern. This information is necessary to establish whether all species that ought to be considered of concern are identified in Forest plans.

Based on these objectives, we articulated five primary monitoring questions for terrestrial animal species and their habitats. While the questions are general in nature and would be useful in any natural resource management situation, they are stated below in a form that relates directly to NFMA plans:

1. Are species, habitat, and community objectives being achieved consistent with outcomes anticipated in plans?

This question is directed at those species, habitats, and communities that are identified as being of concern or interest in Forest plans, and for which specific outcomes are stated or implied. These outcomes may be quite general (e.g., maintain breeding populations in every fourth-order watershed) or very specific (e.g., maintain over time four snags per acre >20 inches dbh in managed areas). Translation of outcomes into measurable terms is necessary for meaningful monitoring under this question.

2. Are species, habitats, and communities responding to specific management activities and the effects of those activities as anticipated in plans?

USDA Forest Service Gen. Tech. Rep. RMRS-GTR-161. 2005

5

As with question 1, this question is directed at those species, habitats, and communities that are identified as being of concern or interest in Forest plans, and for which specific outcomes are stated or implied. However, the question here is not whether overall outcomes are being achieved as in question 1. Rather, here we are asking if specific management activities are having the effects that were anticipated. For example, if certain nest sites are buffered from recreation activities during the breeding season, we might ask if those sites have higher reproductive success than sites that are not protected from recreation activities.

3. What are the status and trends of species, habitats, and communities of concern and interest for which there are not specific anticipated outcomes in the Forest plan?

This question addresses species, habitats, or communities that are identified to be of concern or interest, but for which no specific outcomes are stated. These might include invasive species, some sensitive species which are not individually addressed, and some species that are noted to be of special interest but are not the subject of individual outcomes. As an example there may be a general goal in the plan to reduce the rate of spread of invasive species but no specific objective for individual species.

4. What are the status and trends of broader measures of biological diversity and ecosystem change for which there are not specific anticipated outcomes in the Forest plan?

The intent here is to look at a broader array of species, habitats, and communities than is addressed in questions 1-3. This will provide information on issues such as diversity and broad changes in distributional patterns that may result from the ongoing effects of multiple stressors. This would include unexpected changes in species not tracked under the other monitoring questions.

5. What are the mechanisms underlying change in habitats and communities, and species responses to changes in ecological conditions?

This question looks at actual mechanisms underlying changes in habitats, communities, and species. As an example, we could ask what effect the composition, structure, and landscape pattern of habitats have on reproductive and/or survival rates of a species. Studies designed to look at underlying mechanisms may be considered by some to be "research" rather than "monitoring." Regardless of the term used, such studies require designs that look at controls and treatments, with alternative treatments as a desirable feature.

Selection of Ecosystem Elements to Monitor

The first step in moving from a series of broad questions to a feasible monitoring program is to determine those ecosystem elements (e.g., communities, habitats, species) that will be selected for monitoring under each of the monitoring questions. Once the elements are chosen, then specific characteristics of those elements (e.g., number, spatial extent, vital rates) are identified as measures, and monitoring designs are developed to provide estimates of those measures. The next two sections provide guidance for the selection of ecosystem elements and measures.

Selection of elements to be monitored requires consideration of information regarding management issues as well as information about the elements under consideration. The following types of knowledge are important to the selection of elements.

- The dominant management issues faced by the land manager.
- The major uncertainties associated with the most important management issues.
- The dominant biological taxa that are deemed important by society and/or are ecologically associated with critical uncertainties.
- The characteristics of species that will determine whether they will effectively reflect change in the environment. In particular an understanding of the response of the taxa to directional change in the environment and whether:

  o response to change is expected to occur in a predictable direction over the range of expected environmental change.
  o response is expected to be large (significant) and measurable relative to the environmental variation.
  o background variation in the species population dynamics are not likely to obscure any directional signal.
  o the time lag between environmental change and change in the species will be short and constant across time. That is, it is important to detect changes before it is too late to correct observed problems.
  o species detectability is adequate to allow effective determination of trends.

The following criteria describe ecosystem elements that should be selected for monitoring under each of the monitoring questions. Application of these criteria would

6

USDA Forest Service Gen. Tech. Rep. RMRS-GTR-161. 2005

narrow the list of elements that might be selected under each monitoring question, but that list will likely still contain more elements than can be addressed with limited monitoring resources. Further prioritization of these elements will almost always be necessary. One approach would be to set priorities by first meeting legal obligations, then focusing on elements at high risk that might be strongly influenced by management, and then elements that have direct or indirect effects on many other elements. Ecosystem modeling may help focus on those elements that are most likely to be strongly influenced by ongoing ecological processes and management, or that are likely to have strong influences on other elements. For example, modeling would help identify species that will be both negatively and positively influenced by widespread fuel reduction projects.

Preliminary selection criteria follow for each of the five monitoring questions.

1. Are species, habitat, and community objectives being achieved consistent with outcomes anticipated in plans?

Criteria for species to be monitored

- Species at risk/of concern for which there is enough knowledge to make projections in the Forest plan.
- Species of social/economic interest for which objectives are established in the Forest plan.
- Species that play a significant role in maintaining the structure and processes of dominant ecosystems affected by management.
- Species that are strongly affected by management.
- Species selected under surrogate concepts to help establish conservation approaches in the Forest plan.
- Exotics that are thought to have a strong ecological influence (for example, on disturbance processes or on other species).

Criteria for habitats and communities to be monitored

- All habitats and communities (including their composition, structure, distribution, and landscape pattern) for which desired conditions and objectives are established as part of the broad ecosystem approach adopted in the Forest plan.
- Habitats and communities that are at risk/of concern or of interest and for which there is enough knowledge to make projections in the Forest plan. These would include rare/unique/irreplaceable habitats and communities and other habitats and communities that support high levels of biodiversity.

2. Are species, habitats, and communities responding to specific management activities and the effects of those activities as anticipated in plans?

The criteria for species, habitats, and communities to be monitored under question 2 are the same as under question 1, except that (1) more emphasis is given here to those species, habitats and communities that are most responsive to dominant management activities and effects, and (2) monitoring focuses on species, habitats and communities for which there is greatest risk and uncertainty.

3. What are the status and trends of species, habitats, and communities of concern and interest for which there are not specific anticipated outcomes in the Forest plan (e.g., exotics, some sensitive species, species of special interest)?

Criteria for species, habitats and communities to be monitored under question 3 are similar to those for question 1. However, those addressed under question 3 are not individually addressed in the Forest plans and are likely to be less well known.

4. What are the status and trends of broader measures of biological diversity and ecosystem change for which there are not specific anticipated outcomes in the Forest plan?

Criteria for species to be monitored

- Individual species and groups of species that, taken together, serve as indicators of broad patterns of diversity and response to management and other changes in ecological conditions.

Criteria for habitats and communities to be monitored

- Most important elements to be monitored are already included under questions 1, 2, and 3. However, it might also be important to provide for direct measures of ecosystem processes (e.g., hydrology, nutrient cycling) under this question.

5. What are the mechanisms underlying change in habitats and communities, and species responses to changes in ecological conditions?

Studies to determine underlying causes of change will likely be intensive and expensive. Thus, they should be

USDA Forest Service Gen. Tech. Rep. RMRS-GTR-161. 2005

7

directed at key ecosystem elements that are at high risk, that have significant impact on overall systems, and/or whose response to management is highly uncertain. These broad criteria should be considered in conjunction with the specific species, habitat, and community criteria given below.

Criteria for species to be monitored
- Species of concern.
- Species that play a significant role in maintaining the structure and processes of dominant ecosystems affected by management.
- Species selected under surrogate concepts to help establish conservation approaches in the Forest plan.
- Exotics that are thought to have a strong ecological influence (for example, on disturbance processes or on other species).

Criteria for habitats and communities to be monitored
- Habitats and communities (including their composition, structure, distribution, and landscape pattern) whose response to management is uncertain.
- Habitats and communities that are at risk/of concern.

Selection of Measures for the Ecosystem Elements

Once the elements (species, communities, habitats) that are to be monitored are selected, we must determine the appropriate measure to respond to the monitoring objective. Below we discuss population, community, and habitat measures. If several different measures are appropriate in any given application, priority should be given to measures that are commonly used, easily employed, have standard methods for collection, relate most closely to the issue motivating monitoring, and are least expensive to measure.

Population and community measures

We categorize monitoring measures into two groups—population measures and community measures. Population measures are those that would be applied to individual species, while community measures apply to multiple species within a community. It is critical to distinguish between population and community measures and to understand the strengths and weaknesses of each. Population measures are known to be sensitive to change, while community measures are quite insensitive. However, community measures by definition integrate over multiple species and thus may be more meaningful in some circumstances. Table 4 lists the

pluses and minuses of five categories of population measures: (1) presence / absence, (2) abundance or density, (3) vital rates, (4) range distribution, and (5) genetic measures; as well as two categories of community measures: (1) diversity and (2) integrity.

When selecting population measures, there is often a choice between direct measures and indices. Examples of direct measures would include estimates of population numbers, or estimates of vital rates from direct observations such as clutch size and adult survival. In contrast, indices are measures that may be correlated with population size or vital rates but are not direct observations of those parameters. Track and scat counts are common examples of indices. In general using direct measures of population parameters is preferred. However, given the logistic difficulty and cost prohibitive nature of direct measures, indices may be usable alternatives (Caughley 1977, McKelvey and Pearson 2001). If indices are used, their inherent weaknesses must be understood. For broad-scale monitoring, the relationships between indices and the parameters they represent must be predictable across space and time; for example, a good index would be one that increases in a predictable way as the numbers of a species increases. It is important to understand any systematic bias in indices. For example, pellet counts for deer are highest in the areas in which they defecate and may not accurately represent overall patterns of habitat use. It is also important to understand the mechanistic relationship between an index and the parameter it represents, and factors that might cause that relationship to vary. For example, snowshoe hare scats should provide a better index of population size than habitat condition. More hares should produce more scats whereas the relationship between habitat and population may be strongly influenced by exogenous factors such as weather. However, even scat numbers should be interpreted with caution. Scat counts can be affected by decomposition rates and variation in diet in addition to population density.

Habitat measures

Species respond to habitat quality, quantity, and configuration at multiple scales. Most habitat measures are designed to assess vegetation composition and structure within a stand or patch and result in a quantitative measure of habitat quality within that area. In addition to responding to the quality of habitat at discrete sites, many species also respond to the configuration of habitat over larger areas. Additional measures are needed to characterize and monitor this configuration including measures such as patch size, patch density, edge density, and nearest neighbor distance.

8

USDA Forest Service Gen. Tech. Rep. RMRS-GTR-161. 2005

Table 4—Population and community measures that may be employed in a monitoring program.

Population measures:

1) Presence/Absence
General description of approach: Sample to determine presence of an organism at sample points. Demonstrating presence requires only concrete proof of the species' existence at a location, while demonstrating absence requires knowledge of the probability of detecting the organism given its presence. P / A detection methods at plots can be effective as long as the probability of detecting an animal (given that it is present) is constant through time or can be estimated based on field data.

2) Abundance or Density
General description of approach: Abundance and density can be formally estimated using a class of well-developed techniques, or it can be monitored indirectly through an index related to abundance (Lebreton and others 1992; Pollock and others 1990; Otis and others 1978). Formal estimates can range from the simple Lincoln Peterson index with only three parameters, to complex models that account for other environmental, social, time, demographic, and location parameters. Typically the cost of obtaining an abundance estimate increases proportionally to the number of parameters estimated; likewise precision is often gained proportionate to cost and can approach a plateau where incremental improvements in precision become increasingly expensive. Because these measures can be expensive, abundance is often inferred through an index. Density is simply abundance per area; however, estimates of density are complicated by the need to estimate the effective area being sampled.

3) Vital Rates
General description of approach: Vital rates are age-specific birth and death rates or emigration/immigration rates. Here we will only address birth and death (in rare cases, immigration and emigration will be of direct interest and appropriate literature should be consulted to examine the use of these measures). Techniques are available for both estimates of vital rates and indices of those rates. Vital rates are a cornerstone of population viability analysis and an understanding of vital rates provides insight into population status (Beissinger and McCullough 2002, Franklin and others 2004). Depending on life history, monitoring of vital rates often provides a better measure of trend than measures of abundance. Furthermore, understanding how vital rates change in response to management provides insight into potential mediation or mitigation, although demography is also influenced by factors such as weather (Raphael and others 1996) that are beyond the control of managers. Demographic sensitivity or elasticity analysis can aid in identifying the appropriate vital rate to monitor.

4) Range Distribution Measures
General description of approach: Geographic range is estimated through either presence/absence measures or through collaboration with other monitoring systems (such as Breeding Bird Survey) that allow the spatial extent of the species occupied range to be tracked over time. Sometimes the goal of monitoring will be to determine whether the range of a species is expanding, contracting, or remaining relatively constant. This is often the case with exotic or endangered species, where the goal may be to compare the current geographic range to historic distributions. Some theory would suggest that geographic range is relatively sensitive to population status and therefore a species' distribution may provide an effective indication of status (Maurer 1994).

5) Genetic Measures
General description of approach: It is important to distinguish between the use of genetics as a tool to bolster other monitoring efforts (e.g., to verify presence/absence of a species) and the use of genetic parameters as measures in and of themselves. For instance, determining the presence of a species and subsequently counting the number of unique individuals from scat or hair (non-invasive genetic sampling) surveys exemplifies how genetics can add to current monitoring practices. In addition to this function of providing defensible monitoring results, there are several genetic parameters that can serve as measures on their own. The three direct genetic parameters most likely to be of practical value will be: (a) change in allelic diversity in the population over time, (b) detection of a genetic population bottleneck, and (c) change in effective population size estimated from changes in gene frequencies across time.

Community Measures:

1) Diversity Measures
General description of approach: Species diversity is expressed through measures of species richness and species evenness. Species richness may be based on repeated measures of species composition (e.g. presence/absence of taxa). Species evenness requires abundance data. Measures of species diversity have been employed in research settings to examine particular questions in community and ecosystem ecology. However, in a management setting it is difficult to determine relationships between measures of diversity and specific management problems. Challenges include identifying the taxa groups to monitor (e.g. groups identified by trophic relationships, functional relationships, taxonomic relationships, etc.), the choice of diversity index, and interpretation of results. These challenges have limited the utility of these measures in resource management monitoring.

2) Integrity Measures
General description of approach: Karr and Dudley (1981) define biological integrity as the "capability of supporting and maintaining a balanced, integrated, adaptive community of organisms having a species composition, diversity, and functional organization comparable to that of the natural habitat of the region." The concept of biological integrity has evolved in response to perceived flaws in the biological diversity measures. Estimating biological integrity requires asking if conditions on the landscape today are similar to conditions present at a specific instance in history or to a nearby "natural" baseline habitat. Because this measure would rely on comparing a measure of diversity across space or time, it is subject to the same difficulties described for diversity measures.

USDA Forest Service Gen. Tech. Rep. RMRS-GTR-161. 2005

9

10

USDA Forest Service Gen. Tech. Rep. RMRS-GTR-161. 2005

Chapter 3

Creating an Integrated Monitoring Program

In discussing monitoring approaches that would be needed to respond to the five key monitoring questions, we found it useful to define three types of monitoring: targeted, context, and cause-and-effect (figure 1). This section describes each type of monitoring, discusses the strengths of each, and provides guidance on relative levels of emphasis that would go into each type of monitoring in different situations. It explores how the three types of monitoring can work together and concludes with a description of the integration of population and habitat data.

Categories of Monitoring

Targeted monitoring

Monitoring that looks directly at effects of management is the subject of the 1982 NFMA regulations and is also the primary type of monitoring required in EMS. In this document we refer to this first type of monitoring as TARGETED monitoring. Targeted monitoring is done to answer a specific question about a population, habitat

feature, or species group of interest. We use targeted monitoring to determine whether the Forest plan objectives for a species are being met and whether management actions are having expected effects. For example, we may monitor to determine whether marten populations decline in areas of forest thinning as would be predicted by understandings of marten habitat use.

Targeted monitoring would be used to directly address monitoring questions 1, 2, and 3.

Cause-and-effect monitoring

Targeted monitoring, as described above, informs us concerning trends in specific ecosystem elements and whether anticipated effects are occurring. However, it generally does not inform us about the causes of observed trends and what alternative management strategies we should pursue if effects are not as anticipated. To better understand how management should be changed, we need to understand actual mechanisms underlying changes in habitats, communities, and species. Monitoring designed to look at underlying mechanisms generally

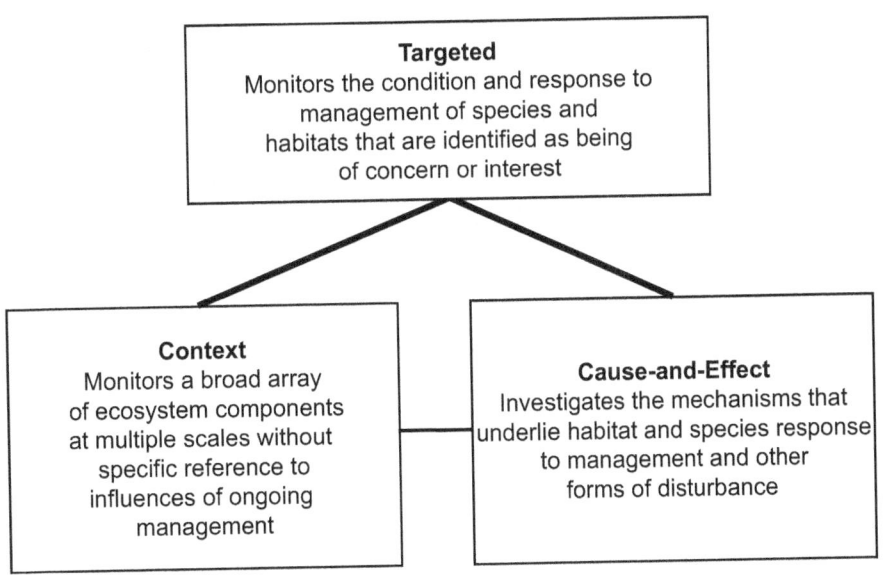

Figure 1—Three types of monitoring described in this report.

USDA Forest Service Gen. Tech. Rep. RMRS-GTR-161. 2005

11

requires designs that include controls and alternative treatments. We refer to this second type of monitoring as CAUSE-AND-EFFECT monitoring. Cause-and-effect monitoring directly addresses monitoring question 5.

Context monitoring

In addition to direct monitoring of Forest plans and monitoring of underlying mechanisms, another less obvious form of monitoring may also be very important. CONTEXT monitoring is intended to look at a broad array of ecosystem components without specific reference to those components that are expected to be affected by current management activities. Over the long term, such monitoring may be extremely important in allowing us to look at (1) cumulative effects of various types of activities on ecosystems; (2) effects that result from the interaction of our activities with broader changes (e.g., global climate change); and (3) effects on ecosystem components that we had not expected to be influenced by our management (Karieva and Wennergren 1995, Tilman and others 1994). For Forest plan monitoring, it provides a context within which the results of targeted monitoring can be evaluated. Context monitoring addresses monitoring question 4 and provides background information that will aid in the interpretation of the other monitoring questions.

Strengths of Different Monitoring Types

Targeted monitoring

The following are primary strengths of targeted monitoring:

- It is focused on indicators that are selected because of risk, concern, or interest.
- It can be focused on elements that are most likely to change.
- It can be tied directly to management objectives.
- Because of its focus, it is relatively efficient and cost effective.
- It has a high probability of detecting targeted changes.

Targeted monitoring directly examines change in selected measures (e.g., population size) for a particular species, habitat, community, or ecosystem. Properly implemented, targeted monitoring meets requirements of the 1982 administrative rules promulgated under NFMA.

Targeted monitoring allows flexibility in the selection of indicators for which technically reliable and cost-effective monitoring methods exist, and that are expected to be sensitive to management actions. However, the implied assumption that observed changes are directly due to management activities is also the weakness of targeted monitoring. Unless trend data collected in a targeted monitoring program are evaluated in light of regional or global trends (context), changes may be erroneously attributed to a management activity. For example, the decline of lynx on a Forest may, or may not, be due to a particular management activity. Rather, the trend may be due to global climate changes or to a natural decline due to population cycling. Therefore, while targeted monitoring is well suited to tracking the trends of specific indicators, such as MIS, unless the results can be placed within a broader context, proper interpretation of these results is impossible. Full understanding of causes of change also requires cause-and-effect monitoring.

Cause-and-effect monitoring

The following are primary strengths of cause-and-effect monitoring:

- It allows investigation of assumptions used in land/resource planning models.
- It can be focused on ecosystem elements that are of greatest interest or concern.
- It leads to greater understanding of mechanisms underlying patterns.
- These understandings can be used to modify management.
- It may provide predictive capability, allowing management to refine future choices.

Cause-and-effect monitoring provides understanding of the causal mechanisms underlying observed trends. Such understanding is necessary so that managers will know what actions to take to change unfavorable trends.

Cause-and-effect monitoring integrates monitoring with research. Historically, the determination of cause-and-effect has been delegated to separate research efforts. In many cases this may still be the best approach, but a tie between standard time-series monitoring and research provides special opportunities to improve understanding and to develop mechanistic understanding of trends at spatial and temporal scales larger than generally can be achieved through separate research efforts.

Generally, research is only weakly coupled to management activities. Therefore, research that is directly applicable to current activities in the area where an unfavorable trend has been observed is often lacking. If, upon observation of an unfavorable trend, a highly directed research program is initiated, the subsequent results will likely take substantial time to produce. Frequently, the lag between the results of directed research and the need to take action leads to actions being taken prior to completion of the research. Management actions therefore often do not benefit from ongoing research and lack the defensibility associated with relevant, peer reviewed information. Ideally, with cause-and-effect monitoring, we build experimental design into the management itself and monitor consequences of specific management actions. Because the research and management occur simultaneously and in the same areas, data obtained will be directly pertinent and the development of causal understandings will be expedited. When cause-and-effect monitoring data are available, not only can management effectively monitor the important element of interest, but management also has knowledge to change the response of the element. As an example, cause-and-effect monitoring led to an understanding that nest sites are the limiting factor for red-cockaded woodpeckers, thus allowing Forests to focus on the maintenance of nest sites and restoration of appropriate conditions within those sites.

The results of cause-and-effect monitoring help identify relationships and often provide the information necessary to alter management in order to reverse unfavorable trends. As a stand alone monitoring strategy, it does not provide information on status and trends of indicators, and so it would not meet agency monitoring obligations.

Context monitoring

The following are primary strengths of context monitoring:

- It is not restricted to selected ecosystem elements.
- It provides status and change information on a wide range of species and habitats.
- It allows detection of unanticipated changes in species and systems.
- It may reflect trends within entire communities of organisms, and allow relatively direct inference to diversity.
- It provides additional context for the interpretation of targeted or cause-and-effect monitoring results.

Context monitoring for terrestrial animals obtains information on population and habitat conditions across broad regions and scales for a variety of species. It is most likely to be based on the application of "omnibus" sampling methods such as breeding bird counts that detect many species simultaneously. The sampling frame and sample density are set based on objectives of detecting as many species as is economically feasible rather than detecting a single species with specific power. Because of the lack of targeting, the data that results for individual species must generally be viewed at broad

scales and over long time periods in order to detect statistically reliable trends. For example, a context monitoring effort could be tailored to provide adequate status and trend information at a regional scale over a 10-year timeframe. When the data from context monitoring are evaluated at these spatial and temporal scales, they can provide scientifically reliable trend data for many species (Manley and others 2004), including some species of concern and interest. Therefore, while they may not provide information to directly evaluate individual management actions, these data can (1) provide a context within which targeted and cause-and-effect monitoring results can be evaluated and interpreted and (2) provide monitoring data on diversity by generating information on broad changes in communities and their component species over time.

Balancing Components in a Comprehensive Monitoring Program

The three types of monitoring are complementary. Each has its own strengths and weaknesses, and each will be most suited to answer particular questions. A program employing all three types of monitoring will be most effective in meeting short- and long-term information needs. All three approaches should be integrated into coordinated monitoring strategies. The appropriate balance among the three will depend on a number of factors. Choices about the balance among the three types of monitoring must be context dependent. We suggest that the balance and priorities of the three monitoring types be established at Regional or higher levels so that appropriate consideration is given to the many monitoring programs that must be conducted across broad spatial extents and institutional boundaries. Assigning priorities at the Regional or higher level will also result in greater consideration of the need for context and cause-and-effect monitoring. At the Forest or District levels, short-term, targeted monitoring needs generally appear most critical.

Figure 2 illustrates how those choices might be made. It provides a framework for managers to evaluate the relative emphasis that would be given to different types of monitoring given the state of knowledge of species, habitat, and communities in a system and levels of risk to those species, habitats, and communities. For example, if we know little about a species, its habitat, community, or ecosystem, it is unlikely that a proper target can be chosen for effective monitoring. If risk is also deemed low, as might be the case in areas with little management activity (figure 2, lower left quadrant),

USDA Forest Service Gen. Tech. Rep. RMRS-GTR-161. 2005

13

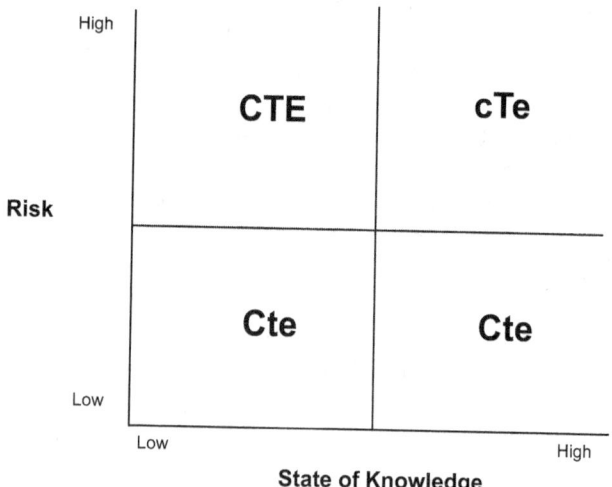

C = Context, T = Targeted, E = Cause and Effect

Figure 2—Graphic showing how risk and state of knowledge could influence relative emphasis among monitoring types. Uppercase letters indicate greater emphasis.

context monitoring would be emphasized. If there were adequate knowledge to know both that elements were at risk, and how those elements might respond to management, then targeted monitoring would predominate (figure 2, upper right quadrant). If risk were somewhat lower, but knowledge well-developed, context monitoring might predominate with the objective of detecting broad trends and unanticipated changes (figure 2, lower right quadrant). If knowledge were poor but risk deemed high, it would be appropriate to allocate significant resources to all three types of monitoring (figure 2, upper left quadrant). In almost all situations, the key decision to be made is level of emphasis to be given to each type of monitoring rather than selecting one type of monitoring to the exclusion of the others.

In an idealized situation, the design of the three monitoring types and the understanding developed from them would be synergistic. Context monitoring would be employed to track trends for many species about which we know little, detect unanticipated change, and track broad-scale trends. These trends would be used as part of the basis for judging significance of targeted monitoring results, as well as identifying populations or habitats that warrant targeted or cause-and-effect monitoring in the future.

Appropriate subjects for targeted monitoring would be selected based on information from context monitoring, information from other sources, knowledge of anticipated management, and ecological modeling. Targeted monitoring would be focused on appropriate indicators and on key locations where effects were anticipated to occur. It would not necessarily always focus on Forest-level status and trends, but would instead look for trends at the most appropriate geographic scale. This might be larger than a single Forest, or be some subdivision of a Forest depending on the question being asked. Where possible, targeted monitoring would use the same sampling techniques as were employed for context monitoring and simply represent an increase in sampling intensity for the selected locations. This would maximize the synergy between targeted and context monitoring. Frequently, however, targeted monitoring would be needed precisely because the techniques used for context monitoring performed poorly for particular species. In other cases, the specific measure identified for targeted monitoring would be different from the measure chosen for context monitoring, thus requiring different sampling techniques. In all situations, however, it is expected that context monitoring would make some contribution to needed targeted monitoring. The level of that contribution will depend on the number of species identified for targeted monitoring and the effectiveness of context monitoring techniques in detecting those species (figure 3).

Cause-and-effect monitoring should be linked to targeted monitoring, if possible by conducting cause-and-effect and targeted monitoring in the same geographic area and timeframe. The subjects for cause-and-effect monitoring should be a subset of those that are being tracked through targeted monitoring. The highest priorities for cause-and-effect monitoring should be those ecosystem elements (species, habitats, and communities) that are expected to be strongly influenced by management decisions, and for which management intervention is possible. Priorities for cause-and-effect monitoring will likely shift over time. Some indicators may be subject only to targeted monitoring for a period of time while we attempt to better understand their status. Based on the results of initial targeted monitoring, these might subsequently be dropped from monitoring programs or be subjected to more intense cause-and-effect monitoring. If cause-and-effect monitoring is successful in determining causal relationships for an indicator, the cause-and-effect portion of a monitoring program for that indicator might be terminated, with targeted monitoring continuing. In this way, cause-and-effect monitoring becomes part of a fluid monitoring program that can be periodically adjusted to reflect updated priorities.

Where context monitoring deals with broad scale variables such as major vegetation types, these may be

14

USDA Forest Service Gen. Tech. Rep. RMRS-GTR-161. 2005

Scenario 1: A small set of species at risk and of concern have been identified, and context monitoring will provide useful information for only a few of these species, thus the contribution of context monitoring to targeted monitoring is limited.

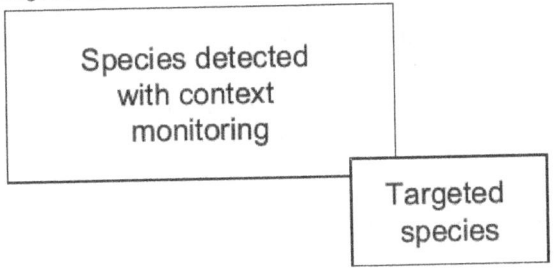

Scenario 2: A large number of species are considered at risk or of concern and interest, many of them are considered low to moderate risk, and context monitoring is deemed an adequate and effective approach to monitoring many of them. The contribution of context monitoring to the objectives of targeted monitoring are substantial.

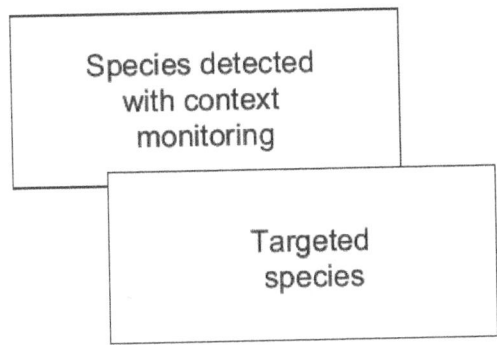

Figure 3—Two possible scenarios for relationships among species subject to context and targeted monitoring.

correlated with variables included in targeted or cause-and-effect monitoring. If these relationships can be established, results from context monitoring may be used to extend the spatial extent of inference of more localized targeted and cause-and-effect monitoring within the area of the context monitoring. Without this extension, the spatial and temporal scope of inference of targeted and cause-and-effect monitoring may be very limited. By working iteratively among the three types of monitoring, it is possible to extend the inference of targeted and cause-and-effect monitoring results, making them considerably more useful to management.

A Case Example to Illustrate Targeted, Cause-and-Effect, and Context Monitoring and Their Relationships

The purpose of this example is to describe how targeted, cause-and-effect and context monitoring interact in a specific situation involving wildlife and habitat management on a National Forest. The example focuses on the Sitka black-tailed deer, a featured species in the Tongass Land Management Plan with high subsistence, recreation, and ecological values.

Information Need 1: What is the population level of deer on Prince of Wales Island, and what is the population trend through time? This information is required to properly regulate the harvest of deer on the island to ensure that hunting demand is provided for without unnecessarily restricting other users. This requires **targeted monitoring** focused in a specific area (Prince of Wales Island) and on a specific management question (what is the population level of deer, and how does it change year to year?).

Information Need 2: How defensible are the deer-habitat relationships contained in the Tongass Land Management Plan? This information is required to test and validate the assumptions, models, and management hypotheses used to address deer concerns and objectives in the plan. For example, it was assumed that as cutover forest areas reached canopy closure, understory

USDA Forest Service Gen. Tech. Rep. RMRS-GTR-161. 2005

15

vegetation would decline with a subsequent reduction in carrying capacity for deer. It was predicted that this effect could be mitigated by thinning treatments to slow the process of canopy closure. This requires **cause-and-effect monitoring**, carried out as administrative studies and demonstration projects, to test and validate the predicted relationships.

Information Need 3: If trends in deer and habitat relationships are not as predicted in the plan, is this because: (1) our models and assumptions are faulty, or (2) background change, unrelated to our management actions, is confounding the results? For the past 25 years or so, Sitka black-tailed deer experts have assumed that periodic severe (deep snow) winters exert an over-riding control on deer populations. Based on past climate data, such winters are assumed to occur every decade or so. In deer-habitat models for Sitka black-tailed deer, snowfall figures prominently in determinations of habitat quality and availability. In Alaska today, however, there is mounting evidence of a warming trend, which affects the probability and frequency of severe winter events, which in turn affects dynamics of the deer population and its habitat. **Context monitoring** that assesses Region-wide changes to deer populations is essential to sort out the effects of background change (e.g., milder winters) from the effects associated with local management actions designed to affect habitat.

USDA Forest Service Gen. Tech. Rep. RMRS-GTR-161. 2005

Chapter 4

Sampling Design and Statistical Considerations and Guidelines

Once the monitoring questions, elements, measures and approaches are determined, several specific design and statistical considerations must be addressed. This chapter highlights key considerations for creating a successful monitoring program. These include the ecological and management context within which monitoring will occur, appropriate scale, limitations, statistical/design consideration, and appropriate levels of review.

Ecological and Management Context

In developing monitoring recommendations at a national level, it's important to acknowledge ecological and management situations that differ greatly across the National Forests and Grasslands. Primary differences can be described in the following areas:

- Levels of management activity—National Forests and Grasslands differ greatly in both historical and current levels of management. Forests in the northeast and southeast were generally highly disturbed during the first period of European settlement beginning in the 1600s, and most of the eastern forest has developed as secondary regeneration. Heavy disturbance occurred later in western forests, with major levels of timber harvest not occurring until the mid-20th century in many areas. Some western forests have still not been subject to significant management disturbance, although they may have been changed by fire protection, grazing, etc. Current levels of management activity also differ greatly and may influence judgments about necessary levels of monitoring activities. Where Forests and Grasslands have not been significantly disturbed, conditions are similar to the natural range of variation, and major management actions are not proposed, less intensive monitoring may be appropriate.
- Geographic continuity—In some Regions, National Forests and Grasslands tend to be isolated and embedded in a matrix of lands of other ownerships (private, state, other federal agency). This is the dominant pattern in the eastern Regions. Western

Regions generally have Forests that are more contiguous to each other. The extent of geographic continuity of NFS lands and partnerships with other agencies will affect sampling design considerations, sample size needs, and the importance of collaborative efforts across multiple ownerships.
- Ongoing monitoring programs—Some Regions participate in broad-scale, cooperative monitoring efforts for selected taxa. The costs and data implications of restructuring an existing, long-term program must be carefully weighed against the potential benefits associated with a new monitoring approach.

Scale Issues

Legal and social structures will often dictate a primary scale of inference for monitoring programs—for NFMA under the 1982 regulations, it is the National Forest. However, status and change monitoring defined by administrative boundaries—project, District, or Forest—will generally have limited utility to inform management. To improve the utility of monitoring, it should be conducted at ecologically meaningful scales that may not match administrative boundaries. For many species this will mean monitoring at the scale of multiple National Forests because the geographic range of the species extends over large geographic areas (e.g., bioregions). Broad-scale, multi-Forest monitoring strategies can still meet obligations for monitoring at the Forest scale if they are conducted at ecologically meaningful scales and designed such that Forest subsets can be evaluated to determine if they are consistent with larger scale trends. Some legally mandated monitoring (e.g., biological opinions issued by the U.S. Fish and Wildlife Service) may require inference at the scale of individual projects, potentially limiting its broader utility. However, ongoing programs of scale-appropriate monitoring may reduce the need for isolated, project-specific monitoring.

Effectiveness of monitoring can often be improved by collecting information at multiple scales through a nested hierarchical system. Multi-scale information aids the understanding of patterns. For example, assume that a

17

Forest has planned to increase elk numbers on the Forest. A number of actions are taken to improve elk habitat (e.g., planting grass, closing roads). Of course, the Forest will be engaged in many other management activities not directed at elk, but that have the potential to affect habitat conditions, such as timber harvest and fuel treatments. A single-scale approach might be to monitor elk numbers at the Forest level. From a planning and legal standpoint, this is the scale of interest in terms of meeting desired conditions. However, measured at this scale, the relationship between elk trends and management actions on the Forest is unknown. Trends could be going up or down due to weather, successional trends within the Forest, hunting patterns on surrounding private land, or a wide variety of other factors, many of which are beyond the scope or the control of Forest management. Thus, additional monitoring at broader scales can provide context for Forest-level patterns. Likewise, monitoring at scales smaller than the Forest might also enhance understanding. For example, monitoring on an individual district with an active road-closure program might reveal differences between district-level and Forest-wide elk habitat use.

Reasonable Expectations of Monitoring Programs

A key consideration in the development of monitoring programs is recognition of limitations of any monitoring effort. Monitoring programs are designed to provide meaningful information, but our knowledge will always be imperfect due to the inherent variability and complexity of ecosystems, the rarity and low detectability of many species, the speed at which lost opportunities become irretrievable, funding constraints, and the inherent limits in our knowledge of ecosystems. Understanding these limitations will help us develop reasonable expectations regarding the information that a monitoring program can provide, and the reliability of that information.

Variability over time

The inherent variability in ecosystems makes it difficult to distinguish annual fluctuations in species abundance from meaningful trends. Most species alter one or more aspects of life history in response to variations in temperature, precipitation, or other climatic factors. Not only does this change the population dynamics of the individual species, but it also affects the relationship of that species to other species that act as competitors, predators, or prey. The level of variability in

populations, even for species of long-lived vertebrates, can be surprisingly high. According to Pimm (1991, as cited in Lande 2002), the abundance of unexploited populations of vertebrates can vary 20 to 80% or more through time. This level of variation makes the results of short-term monitoring programs questionable and significantly influences the interpretation of early results from long-term monitoring programs.

Variability that takes the form of cyclic patterns can also confound our ability to observe trends. As an example, consider snowshoe hares that undergo a stable 10-year population cycle. While an increase or decrease in hares could be detected across a fairly short period of time, it would take at least 20 years to see the 10-year oscillation, several more decades to determine that the dynamics were, in fact, cyclic, and several more yet to determine whether anything unusual was occurring outside the expected range of oscillation. Thus, it should be anticipated that perhaps 50 years might pass before trends were understood in a way that allowed legitimate evaluation of current dynamics.

Development of causal understandings along with status and trend information will likely decrease the amount of time necessary for evaluation of monitoring data. However, the parameters involved in causal relationships may also be subject to intrinsic variability and non-linear patterns. So, development of causal relationships may also require a substantial period of monitoring.

Timeframe of inference

The complexity of ecosystems limits our interpretation of the population status and trend data that monitoring provides. We can document changes that happened during the years the data were collected, but we cannot predict changes that might occur in the future. Projection may be reliable for short periods of time, but the reliability rapidly degrades as we push the projection further into the future. Furthermore, the shorter the period of monitoring, the less reliable the projection that is made from the resulting data. When data are only available from a short period of monitoring, the only possible projection is linear. When data are collected over a longer period, the functional form of the pattern may become apparent and its reliability across space and time evaluated.

Since plant community trends are generally less variable than the population dynamics of animals, it should be possible to forecast habitat data more reliably than population data. Such projections would make use of our understanding of ecological processes and the relationship of these processes to climate. Nevertheless, long-term forecasting is limited by our knowledge of the effects of factors such as global climate change and the spread of invasive species.

Geographic area of inference

We must also consider geographic limitations to monitoring information. The geographic area over which we can draw inferences from any data set, including monitoring data, is dictated by the area within and the process by which sample sites are selected (sampling frame). If sites selected for status and change monitoring are selected in a systematic or randomized manner within a given National Forest, then data from that sample can be used to make inferences about status and change on the National Forest. Extrapolation of these monitoring results from one Forest to another, however, is tenuous. Our confidence in such an extrapolation may be increased slightly by carefully describing the ecological and management situation in which the data are collected and extrapolating results only to similar situations. However, such extrapolations will always be weakened by inevitable dissimilarities between situations. One of the strengths of context monitoring is that it is implemented using similar methodologies across broad spatial scales and over time so there is less need for extrapolation of data.

Sample Design

Two key components of a credible monitoring program are protocols for data collection and an overall sample design. A protocol establishes how data are to be collected at each sample point, while the overall design determines where the samples will be located and the timing of data collection. National Forests and Grasslands frequently ensure that their monitoring programs use a prescribed field protocol, but it is rare that the field methods are embedded within an explicitly stated randomized sample design. Without a randomized sample design, it is not possible to determine whether the monitoring data are representative of an entire area of interest, or only certain aspects of it, such as certain habitats or management situations. When data are collected without a randomized sample design, there is no valid basis for making inferences from the sample to the population of interest, and there also is no valid basis for assessing precision of the estimated population parameters.

For every specific monitoring plan, a sample design should be selected that best meets the monitoring objectives. Samples must provide for an unbiased representation of the population of interest. For context monitoring, the sampling frame must include all cover types within the desired area of inference, and the sample design must provide for good spatial dispersion of samples across the sampling frame. The sampling frame for targeted monitoring should represent all potential habitats for the species throughout the area of inference. Even habitats thought to have low potential to support a species should be included in sampling in order to avoid biasing the resulting estimate. For cause-and-effect monitoring, the sample design will, in most cases, be based on treatment and control blocks, and include replicates (that is, multiple blocks in which management actions occur and similar blocks where no actions are taken). For all types of monitoring, the sample size must be adequate to detect the desired degree of change ("effect size") with the desired level of confidence.

The sample design for individual species monitoring must also take into account specific aspects of a species' life history and habitats so that data collection can be optimized and results properly interpreted. Examples include home range size, territoriality (or conversely, social clumping), seasonal use patterns, and natural population fluctuations. Home range size and territoriality (or social clumping) influence plot size and the spacing between plots within the sampling frame, as well as interpretations of habitat use patterns. Seasonal use patterns could determine the optimal time of year for detecting a species, interpreting fluctuations within a season related to the appearance of young of the year, and interpreting observed occurrence or habitat use data. For context monitoring of multiple species, the sample design should include sampling several times over the potential sampling season so that data are not biased toward early or late seasonal species, and the timing of sampling should either be simultaneous across all plots, or randomized such that certain habitats and areas are not preferentially sampled either early or late in the season.

The magnitude of change that we desire to detect also drives the design of a monitoring program. Monitoring plans should specify the amount of change that is considered to be ecologically significant or otherwise deemed appropriate as an evaluation checkpoint or threshold. Natural population fluctuations must be considered when specifying a desired effect size. For example, if a 20% change in population is within the range of normal fluctuations, it may not be necessary to detect a 20% change in population for management purposes. A larger effect size and hence, smaller sample size, might be adequate.

Many sources of error affect the reliability of monitoring data, decreasing the precision of estimates and making it more difficult to reliably detect changes over time. For count and presence/absence data, one of the primary

USDA Forest Service Gen. Tech. Rep. RMRS-GTR-161. 2005

19

sources of error within and among sample periods is the detection probability, which is affected by observer variability, habitat conditions, animal behavior, and detection methods. Estimates of probability of detection can be obtained with well-designed monitoring protocols (MacKenzie and others 2002, Royle and Nichols 2003, Tyre and others 2003).

Although monitoring requirements and information needs exist at the scale of individual National Forests, it is often financially or technically infeasible to obtain the precision and power necessary to detect ecologically meaningful changes in population parameters in a landscape of 1-2 million acres. For many purposes it is more appropriate to design monitoring such that temporal changes can be evaluated over a range of spatial scales, so that changes indicated weakly at the Forest scale can be placed in the context of more precise estimates obtained over broader spatial extents. For some monitoring programs it is also advantageous to design monitoring in a manner that allows data points to be aggregated by a variety of features (strata), such as within a species range, by habitat types, or by type of disturbance (management or natural) so that the data can have maximum utility for a variety of applications. When developing multi-scale monitoring it is critical that measurement methods and quality control standards be standardized across the hierarchy and that the formal linkages among data collected at various spatial scales be incorporated statistically into the overall sample design.

A sample design is not only the heart of every monitoring program, but it also aids in ensuring that the program meets data quality standards. Forest Service monitoring programs will be both more defensible and more efficient if each has a sample design that is specific to the monitoring objectives and natural history of targeted species. Finally, many sampling design options exist for obtaining samples with a known probability, but a good rule of thumb for monitoring programs is to keep the design as simple as possible. The fewer assumptions one has to make in a sampling design, the more robust it is likely to be over time. Risks can be reduced by early consultation with statisticians experienced in sample surveys of populations and habitats.

Sampling Adequacy

Monitoring programs need to be concerned with missing important changes (type II error), as well as falsely concluding that a change has taken place (type I error). Estimates of sample size adequacy should be based on objectives for both statistical power (associated with type II error) and precision (associated with type I

error). Given the short duration of most planning periods (10-15 years) during which population and habitat change must be assessed, precision and power are critical considerations and need to be set high. In the case of targeted monitoring, monitoring should be designed to detect ecologically important effect sizes based on species and plan specific considerations. In most situations, this would translate into power and precision of at least 80% for whatever time period and spatial area is being assessed (e.g., 5, 10, 15 year period). For context monitoring, these same levels of power and precision should be used to assess which species will be adequately sampled by proposed omnibus sampling procedures. If power and precision are lower than these levels, the observed trends form a weak basis for understanding patterns of change and informing management decisions.

When presence/absence data are used, sample sizes needed to reach a given power and precision are generally higher than they would be if abundance data were used. However, abundance data are more expensive to collect than presence/absence data. Cost comparisons should be conducted for context and targeted monitoring to evaluate the relative efficacy of obtaining presence/absence and abundance data for various taxa. Regardless of the type of data collected, monitoring efforts that do not meet these minimum precision and power objectives are not likely to yield useful information on population change.

Review Process

The need for a review process is crucial to ensure that data quality standards are met and that limited monitoring funds are being used as effectively as possible. To that end, we recommend a three-part review process that consists of: (1) an internal agency review after the monitoring design has been developed; (2) an external review after recommendations from the internal review have been incorporated into the design; and (3) periodic supplemental internal reviews to recommend changes in the direction of the monitoring program if needed. We recommend at least one additional formal review four to five years into the monitoring effort.

The internal agency review should consist of a formal review by a Regional team comprised of Regional staff, Station scientists, Forest Supervisors, and species experts. The purpose of this review would be to ensure that the monitoring objectives are clear, the sample design and indicators are sufficient to support the stated objectives, the proposed analytical methods are sound, the implementation is feasible given the topography and available staff, and the monitoring program has incorporated, to the extent

20

USDA Forest Service Gen. Tech. Rep. RMRS-GTR-161. 2005

possible, existing relevant information from previous research or monitoring in the proposed monitoring area. An additional technical review could be done by the Statistical Advisory Group of the Inventory and Monitoring Institute (IMI).

The external review should be coordinated by the Regional office, in partnership with a Forest Service Research Station, which would be responsible for contacting relevant experts for the monitoring program under review. At a minimum, the Regional office should contact personnel at USGS Wildlife Research Center (Patuxent), representatives of all partners in the monitoring effort, and other agency personnel within or near the proposed monitoring program geographic area, such as NPS, BLM, or tribal personnel. The external review should also include university faculty with expertise in biometrics, the relevant species, and the relevant ecosystems. The purpose of this review would be to meet the standards of the U.S. Department of Agriculture Quality of Information Guidelines[3], ensure that all affected parties are adequately informed, and gain advice from qualified persons to improve the design as needed.

Additional reviews should be undertaken over the course of any monitoring program, but as mentioned above, we recommend that at least one additional formal review be incorporated into the review process. The second internal review, conducted after the monitoring program has been in place for a few years, could be carried out by the same groups of people that conducted the initial internal review. This review would ensure that the monitoring program is on the right trajectory for meeting the stated objectives, that data are being entered into the Natural Resource Information System (NRIS), data analysis is underway, and the analytical methods are still appropriate. The review will also provide an opportunity to modify sampling schemes if the present sampling scheme could not be met for logistical reasons. For large, sustained monitoring programs, the use of a standing statistical monitoring group may be helpful.

---

[3] The Department of Agriculture issued revised departmental guidelines for quality of information in 2003 (http://www.ocio.usda.gov/qi_guide/index.html). The guidelines generally call for scientific information released by the Department to be peer reviewed, transparent, and reproducible according to accepted scientific standards. Guidelines are provided for statistical data and for data used in regulatory processes. It is likely that monitoring data would fall under both sets of guidelines.

21

USDA Forest Service Gen. Tech. Rep. RMRS-GTR-161. 2005

Chapter 5

Applying Monitoring to Management

For monitoring to be useful in management decision-making, there must be a formalized adaptive management framework that directs the analysis, evaluation, reporting, and response to monitoring results. This chapter discusses key considerations for adaptive management and analysis of monitoring data in the context of Forest Service management.

Adaptive Management

Adaptive management is the process of designing management actions to gain knowledge about critical uncertainties in our models of management outcomes and to help us choose between alternative models (Walters and Holling 1990). The important difference between trial-and-error learning and adaptive management is that, with the latter, uncertainties that could lead to unforeseen and perhaps irreversible outcomes are explicitly identified. By identifying the uncertainties and then creating management actions so that outcomes can be measured, the resulting actions yield knowledge, even when the outcome is different from what was predicted (Lee 1993).

Targeted, cause-and-effect, and context monitoring should be used in combination to gain knowledge about uncertainties associated with our management. Targeted monitoring focuses on uncertainties about the outcomes of management. Cause-and-effect monitoring focuses on uncertainties about the mechanisms by which proposed management, or other possible manipulations, affects species and habitats. Context monitoring focuses on uncertainties concerning the larger context within which proposed management will take place. As an example, we could look at management for white-headed woodpeckers in ponderosa pine forests. Large ponderosa pine snags are considered vital for populations of white-headed woodpeckers, and guidelines have been established for their retention in fuel treatment areas. Targeted monitoring could be conducted to determine if desired densities of white-headed woodpeckers were maintained in areas that were treated according to these guidelines. At the same time, cause-and-effect monitoring could be established to look at the effects of varying densities of snags, live trees, and logs on woodpecker reproduction. Context monitoring could be used to

determine if broad scale changes in populations of several woodpecker species were occurring in correlation with management treatments or other influences such as pine mortality. Comparison of treated and untreated landscapes might also be possible through context monitoring. The combination of these three types of monitoring would provide clear information for any necessary modification of management. Identifying the key areas of uncertainty would help determine appropriate emphasis in the monitoring program.

Evaluation of Targeted, Context, and Cause-and-Effect Data

The evaluation of management outcomes and the timely use of new information by decision makers are critical components of the adaptive management process. Monitoring data are neutral—they simply paint a picture. It is land managers and scientists who must determine how monitoring data are interpreted to represent success, concern, or failure in meeting management objectives.

Periodically, the data from targeted, context, and cause-and-effect monitoring programs must be evaluated both separately and together to determine if desired conditions are being met and whether specific knowledge gaps have been sufficiently filled to adjust or reaffirm management actions. The evaluation of targeted and context monitoring data should be based on pre-selected "threshold" or "trigger point" values that represent desired or undesirable conditions for each measure. For cause-and-effect monitoring, evaluation should focus on values that represent ecologically significant levels of response by species or habitat conditions to management actions.

The terms "thresholds" and "trigger points" are often used to indicate parameter values of concern and cause for action, but the evaluation of monitoring results should also recognize when desired conditions are being met. Thus, we suggest that a more neutral term, "evaluation checkpoints," be used. Checkpoints can be based on a variety of consideration, including ecological thresholds, management direction, and legal requirements.

Well-developed checkpoints provide a strong foundation for a considered management response to monitoring

USDA Forest Service Gen. Tech. Rep. RMRS-GTR-161. 2005

23

results. Ideally, pre-negotiated management responses to checkpoints would be described in the monitoring plan, but this rarely occurs. More commonly, the appropriate management response is determined after the checkpoint is exceeded. The periodicity of monitoring reports is important since evaluations are likely to take place only when reports are generated.

At the Forest or Regional scales, any problems in a monitoring program can be spotted by producing annual reports outlining planned and actual activities (i.e., how well sampling conformed to the study plan, number of sites sampled, data collected) and presenting a simple summary of results. At 5 to 10 year intervals, it is desirable to conduct detailed data analysis and generate reports for the purposes of evaluating the need for change in either management or the monitoring program. Comprehensive evaluations should include summarization and interpretation of monitoring results at the multi-Forest or Regional scale to ensure that misleading small scale patterns of stasis or change are not mistaken as reliable, sending management in the wrong direction. The 2005 regulations implementing NFMA require evaluations every 5 years. A mix of managers and scientists, as well as collaborators and partners, should be involved in the interpretation of monitoring results at these 5-year time steps and together generate recommendations for appropriate actions by decision makers.

Linkage of Habitat and Population Monitoring

The Forest Service responsibility for wildlife conservation is to provide ecological conditions that are capable of supporting wildlife populations to meet stated objectives. Monitoring information can be used to check our progress toward achieving desired conditions and better define the relationship between populations and ecological conditions, and subsequently refine our notion of the desired conditions toward which we should be managing. The importance of the relationship between population dynamics and ecological conditions was recognized in the 1982 regulation implementing NFMA, which required that changes in population be related to changes in habitat condition. While this specific requirement is eliminated from the 2005 regulations, there are still requirements to monitor "the degree to which on-the-ground management is maintaining or making progress toward the desired conditions and objectives for the plan" (36 CFR 219.6 (b)(2)(iii). In the remainder of this discussion we use the term "habitat" instead of "ecological conditions," but it is intended in the sense of the full suite of conditions that influence wildlife populations.

Because of the complexities inherent in monitoring animal populations, it is often proposed that we monitor only habitat rather than monitoring both habitat and populations. However, habitat monitoring alone has limited usefulness in predicting wildlife populations for several reasons:

- Our understanding of wildlife-habitat relationships is poor for most species.
- Wildlife species may be affected by properties of the larger landscape, outside the area being measured.
- The habitat variables measured may be chosen for logistical reasons rather than because they are the best indicators of ecological conditions for targeted species. For instance, red-cockaded woodpecker populations are known to be strongly influenced by the availability of nest cavities, yet nest cavities are not likely to be assessed in a general habitat monitoring scheme.
- The disturbance history (e.g. fire, timber harvest) of an area may influence population size, especially where wildlife species are not mobile and/or where populations are fragmented.
- Current disturbances, such as recreational use, may not affect the physical features of an area but can limit or exclude occupancy by species sensitive to human presence.
- The wildlife species of concern may be influenced by population size of other prey, predator, mutualistic, or competitor wildlife species.
- Population-limiting processes may occur elsewhere for migratory or seasonally mobile species.
- Intrinsic factors, such as disease or parasites, may cause declines in wildlife species that are not predicted by habitat. The general amphibian decline of the past several decades is a good example in which population changes would have been poorly predicted by habitat monitoring alone.

In a limited number of situations it may be appropriate to monitor only habitat and project population responses to that habitat. For example, tracking proportions of gross habitat types, as from satellite imagery, may be useful for habitat specialists and species whose distribution or abundance is generally limited by habitat. To be useful, it must be possible to remotely sense an attribute of the habitat that limits the species. For example, early successional stages of forested habitats are usually easily detected with satellite imagery, and a loss of early-successional habitat will inevitably produce a decline in a broad suite of species associated with early succession.

24

USDA Forest Service Gen. Tech. Rep. RMRS-GTR-161. 2005

For species that are not in decline and whose population levels have been demonstrated to be strongly tied to habitat, this information may suffice. However, for the many reasons listed in the bullets above, a more informed understanding requires us to effectively relate population data to habitat data.

Where habitat and population data are being collected to refine our understanding of their relationship, several factors must be considered:

- Effects of external influences on populations, such as those mentioned above, are likely to introduce variability into the habitat/population relationship.
- Collection of habitat data must be consistent with the spatial scale at which species respond to habitat.
- Different levels of habitat data specificity may be needed for collection with different population measures:

  o Predictions of presence/absence for wildlife can be based on broad and correlative habitat variables;
  o Predictions of population change should be based on variables closely tied to factors inducing population change; and
  o Predictions for survival and reproduction should be based on habitat attributes thought to directly influence survival and reproduction, e.g., food availability.

Considerations for relating populations and habitat differ among the three monitoring types.

In context monitoring, species population parameters tend to be those that are easiest to collect (e.g., presence/absence), and the same sample points tend to be used for multiple taxa. Statistical habitat relationships can be generated by correlating either the number of organisms or the presence of organisms with the collected habitat variables. For some taxa, appropriate habitat data may consist of major vegetation types close to the sample point. For example, presence/absence of bird species with small home ranges may be correlated with major vegetation types within 0.1 miles of the sample point. Correlations may be enhanced by including variables representing understory structure and composition in addition to the major vegetation type. However, for other taxa such as mammals with large home ranges, this area may be too small for appropriate population-habitat correlations. For still other taxa such as amphibians and some small mammals, knowledge of very localized and specific features such as logs may be needed to produce meaningful correlations. Finally, for some taxa, we do not know *a priori* the scale at which habitat data must be collected for correlation with population data. So, multi-scale habitat data will likely be required in order to develop population-habitat correlations for multi-species context monitoring.

Determining habitat variables to be collected in conjunction with targeted monitoring is likely simpler because it is directed at individual species or species groups in particular situations. For example, targeted monitoring of habitat conditions specific to the species at various scales would be clearly identified and monitored spatially and temporally coincident with population monitoring. Cause-and-effect monitoring also has clearly identified species, areas of interest, management activities, and predicted population and habitat responses. For both targeted and cause-and-effect monitoring it is important that wildlife and habitat observations are co-located within home-ranges of the targeted species. Selection of habitat variables should be based on conditions known or suspected to influence wildlife populations. Existing habitat relationships models are one way to identify the key habitat and limiting variables.

25

USDA Forest Service Gen. Tech. Rep. RMRS-GTR-161. 2005

Chapter 6

Organizational Considerations

Implementation of effective monitoring that is useful in meeting Forest Service management goals requires changes in organization and investment patterns. In this chapter we describe what needs to be changed, strategic decisions that need to be made in order to design and implement these changes, and partnerships that can be strengthened to lower costs and increase benefits of monitoring expenditures across land management organizations.

Effective Organizational Structure and Roles

Current situation

Organizations within the Forest Service are not currently structured to facilitate effective design and implementation of programs to monitor terrestrial animals. With the exception of the multi-Forest monitoring programs reviewed in Chapter 1, each National Forest and Grassland is encouraged to conduct independent monitoring programs, but these units are not adequately staffed to carry out comprehensive monitoring. It is assumed that Forest and District personnel are sufficiently trained to design rigorous monitoring programs, and that these same personnel, with additional temporary staff, are able to implement the monitoring programs. There is the expectation that monitoring data can be collected in addition to the accomplishment of other normal duties and fire response duties. In reality, monitoring usually is the first activity to be dropped when other priorities compete for biologists' time. As a result, monitoring efforts vary in intensity and quality from Forest to Forest, fluctuate annually, and are often short-lived.

Moreover, the current structure does not provide the level of statistical expertise that Forest and District biologists need in order to design a monitoring program. As a result, monitoring designs are frequently flawed to the extent that data are unusable or only weak statistical inferences can be made. In many cases, small initial changes in the sampling protocol could have produced robust results. The lack of statistical training or access to statisticians also severely restricts data analysis, with the

outcome that data may be collected for years and never evaluated. The current structure does not generally provide Regional oversight of Forest monitoring programs, so adjacent National Forests and Grasslands develop different approaches to monitoring the same species, and frequently, trends are not comparable between planning units. Moreover, it is difficult for National Forests to orchestrate multi-Forest monitoring efforts, even when such efforts would provide ecologically meaningful data for Forest planning purposes.

The current organizational structure also does not promote collaboration between NFS and R&D, so opportunities to integrate cause-and-effect studies with National Forest management are lost. Moreover, Research Stations may not be aware of the information needs of nearby National Forests, and so they miss opportunities to develop testable hypotheses that would directly benefit the National Forests. In some cases, joint efforts between NFS and R&D are undertaken but ultimately fail because treatments are altered, postponed, or canceled.

Desired condition and organization

The desired goal is to obtain information about terrestrial animals and their habitats that is meaningful for Forest planning and enables the National Forests and Grasslands to "provide for a diversity of plant and animal communities" (NFMA). Ideally, this information would be obtained through monitoring programs that occur at the appropriate ecological scale, are reliably funded, meet data quality standards, are consistent across planning units, and are strategically linked to specific research questions. In order to achieve this condition, we propose two changes in current organizational structure:

(1) strengthen Regional capability to provide leadership, coordination, and oversight of monitoring programs and; (2) strengthen collaboration between NFS and R&D.

Regional Roles—National Forest monitoring programs would benefit greatly if Regional capabilities were expanded to provide the necessary leadership and expertise to obtain meaningful data. Regional offices could provide oversight of existing and proposed monitoring programs, ensure consistency in data collection, identify opportunities to integrate similar monitoring objectives

27

USDA Forest Service Gen. Tech. Rep. RMRS-GTR-161. 2005

on adjacent Forests, and develop effective partnerships with other agencies and organizations. With added staff, Regional offices could also serve as a source of statistical consultation, both for design of Forest monitoring programs and for assistance with data analysis procedures.

A key role of Regional offices should be coordination of any monitoring of terrestrial animals that occurs at multi-Forest or Regional scales. A coordinator should be designated to oversee such programs with responsibility for establishing the multi-Forest sampling frame, acquiring equipment and personnel, providing training to field crews, serving as data steward, and ensuring that data analyses are timely and that the results are made available to all contributing National Forests and partners. This coordination will require a dedicated position, either in the Regional office or elsewhere (see Operational Strategies).

New procedures to fund monitoring at the Regional level should be developed. Currently, most Regions do not have the ability to retain funds at the Regional level for multi-Forest monitoring efforts. Most of the existing multi-Forest monitoring programs were established when off-the-top funding capabilities existed, whereas presently these programs are being pieced together from each contributing National Forest. As a result, these programs are constantly struggling for consistent funding and sampling intensity from year to year. The ability to retain off-the-top funds for monitoring should be reinstated at the Regional level, because ultimately the National Forests would benefit from the efficiencies and quality of information obtained through stable, long-term monitoring efforts.

Regional capabilities can also be strengthened by placing more emphasis on monitoring at the national level. Although NFS is geographically too diverse to operate most monitoring programs at the national scale, national staff could play a significant role in promoting Regional and Forest level monitoring programs. Nationally, the responsibility is to develop policy related to terrestrial animal monitoring, and to market the importance of wildlife monitoring both within the agency and with potential partners. National personnel, including the Chief, should actively demonstrate the potential value of wildlife monitoring to current agency missions, such as the National Fire Plan and the current Off Highway Vehicle (OHV) policy, and strive to build monitoring direction into national regulations and policy regarding Forest planning. National wildlife staff should build alliances with the USGS Status and Trend Monitoring Program, the USGS Wildlife Research Center, and other partners as opportunities arise, and ensure that these partnership opportunities are made available to the

Regions. Currently, these roles are not clearly identified in the WO wildlife staff structure, so wildlife monitoring is not receiving adequate attention nationally. By identifying national roles regarding policy development, marketing, coordination, and partnerships, and ensuring adequate staff to carry out these roles, Regional and Forest level monitoring can be carried out with solid agency support and commitment.

NFS and R&D Collaboration—Close collaboration between NFS and R&D is needed to achieve the goals of enhancing ecological knowledge and increasing understandings of cause-and-effect relationships. Currently, NFS and R&D operate independently except for *ad hoc* cooperative efforts. This independence is appropriate given the distinct missions of each branch. Especially germane is the critical need for independent science, including freedom from the process of establishing policy and consideration of concomitant political issues. Although this separation of missions is necessary in many instances, it is also appropriate to formalize the notion that collaboration within the agency can be useful in response to certain natural resource management situations. Effective monitoring of management activities constitutes one such situation. Collaboration between R&D and NFS is necessary in response to certain monitoring problems. Such collaboration would in no way compromise the independence of the two entities. Field-level line officers from both branches should be assigned the responsibility and authority to design and implement collaborative activities.

Nationally, R&D can play a supportive role by assisting with the development and/or review of monitoring protocols, communicating frequently with national NFS staff regarding collaborative opportunities, and encouraging the Research Stations to build stronger linkages between R&D projects and the information needs of NFS. R&D should evaluate whether the current organization is sufficient to serve these roles effectively. Currently, the National Wildlife Program Leader for Research carries out these and other roles regarding wildlife monitoring.

At the Station level, R&D involvement in Regional and National Forest monitoring programs should be greatly increased. R&D could play key roles in context, targeted, and cause-and-effect studies as illustrated in figure 4. NFS and R&D would collaboratively establish priorities both for context monitoring (boxes on left) and for targeted and cause-and-effect monitoring (boxes on right). Researchers would then take the lead in developing the sample design, selecting variables to measure, and designing the field protocol. NFS would implement context monitoring, whereas R&D would

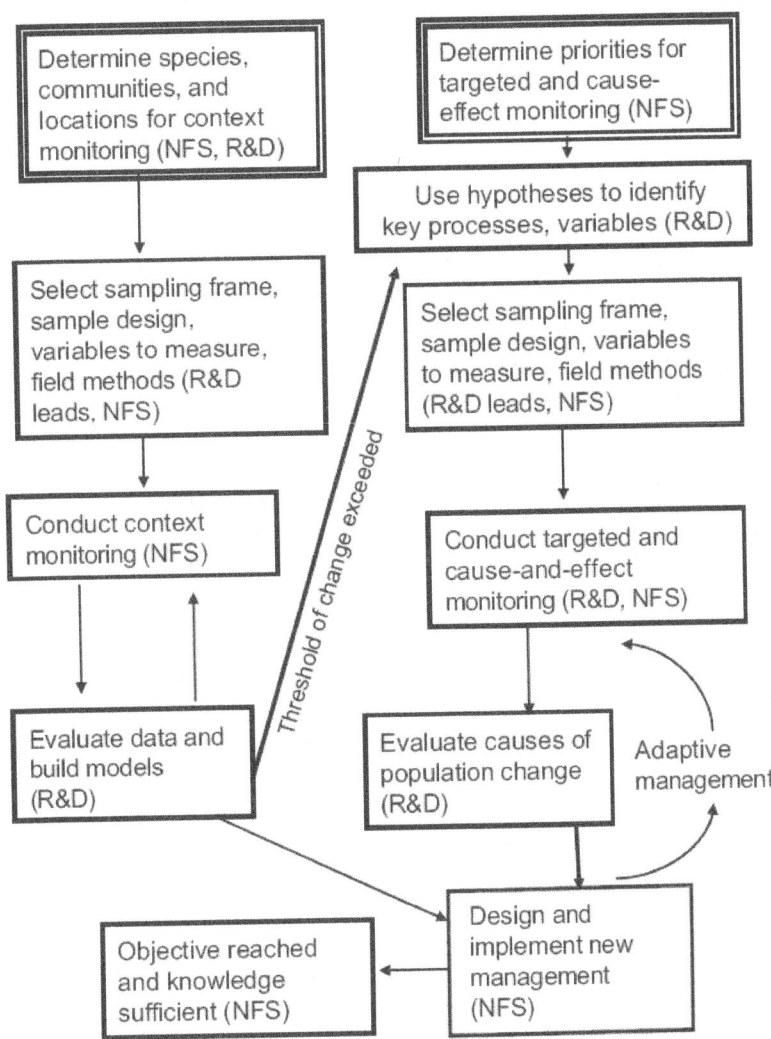

Figure 4—The collaborative roles of R&D and NFS in terrestrial animal monitoring.

conduct cause-and-effect monitoring, and both might be involved with different types of targeted monitoring. Results of context monitoring stimulate further targeted monitoring when thresholds of tolerable change are exceeded. Results of targeted monitoring and cause-and-effect monitoring would be used to adjust or initiate management, and adaptive management would continue until objectives are reached and knowledge of the system is sufficient.

Stronger collaboration between NFS and R&D would likely require additional staffing, since Station scientists are already fully committed to carrying out research project assignments. Stations and Regional offices should consider a doctoral-level shared position per Research Station with primary duties focused on monitoring. A shared position could prove to be an effective way to develop the integration recommended in this report between context, targeted, and cause-and-effect monitoring.

At the National Forest level, Forest line officers and Station project leaders can collaboratively identify a suite of monitoring questions that relate to specific management actions and research strategies. Together, managers and scientists can design and lay out management treatments that implement appropriate experimental design. Results and subsequent analyses would serve to address the initial monitoring questions while simultaneously providing the basis for scientists to advance the ecological understanding needed for informed management.

29

USDA Forest Service Gen. Tech. Rep. RMRS-GTR-161. 2005

There are examples at both the National Forest and Regional level of successful collaboration between NFS and either R&D or university research. The Southern Research Station has conducted a number of studies, funded by the Ouachita National Forest and partners, on the effects of different burn intensities and seasons on wildlife species, which have aided National Forests in the Southern Region to plan future prescribed burns. The University of Montana has initiated four short term cause-and-effect studies related to landbirds, funded by the Northern Region: landscape factors affecting cowbird distribution (Young and Hutto 1999), effects of partial-cut timber harvest (Hutto and Young 2002), effects of thinning and burning in ponderosa pine, and effects of wildfire. Published results of the first two studies are available for incorporation into relevant planning documents.

The Birds and Burns Network conducts targeted monitoring of prescribed fire to examine fire effects on populations and habitats of wildlife in ponderosa pine forests in eight states across the western United States. The target wildlife species are cavity-nesting birds and songbirds (also small mammals at selected locations). This effort has been underway since 2002 and is funded by several sources, including the Joint Fire Sciences Program, several National Forests, the Intermountain Region fire program, and the National Fire Plan. Similarly, Fire and Fire Surrogates was established in 2000 to understand the effects of alternative methods for fuel reduction and forest restoration. Funded by the Joint Fire Sciences program, several National Forests, and numerous other collaborators, the Fire and Fire Surrogates program consists of several long-term studies that use a common experimental design on 13 sites nationwide. Examples of wildlife monitoring projects include forest birds, small mammals, herpetofauna, and two bat species (the eastern red bat [*Lasiurus borealis*] and the eastern pipistrelle [*Pipistrellus subflavus*]). This program has fostered numerous collaborative research and monitoring studies of wildlife as well. While funded independently, each of these projects benefits through an existing experimental framework that includes replicated treatments, random selection of experimental units of a minimum size, and reliable agreements with local managers to insure the maintenance of site conditions through time.

The Pacific Southwest Region has initiated a series of cause-and-effect studies to monitor the effects of off-highway vehicle use on various resources. The Northern Region has worked with R&D to design and implement a DNA based presence/absence survey for multiple species that has led to advances in both science and information pertinent to population management. The Sierra Nevada carnivore study (table 1) is a new collaborative effort between the Pacific Southwest Region and the Pacific Southwest Research Station that shows promise for close coordination between R&D and NFS in the realm of monitoring.

Operational Strategies

Multi-Forest and Regional monitoring programs require substantial coordination to provide for collection and analysis of data with consistent quality and dissemination of reliable information. We propose two alternative approaches for achieving the needed coordination, although other approaches may also exist.

The first approach is the "timber cruising" model, where the design and data collection protocol are established at the Regional scale, and data collection and data quality controls are implemented at the local scale. Under this model, the Regional office would provide the structure for data quality control, while individual units would be responsible for all aspects of implementing the field work, including hiring and training of personnel and performing field reviews of data collection standards. Regional offices would need staff to oversee quality control and collate and analyze incoming data, but the bulk of funds would be dispersed to individual units.

The second approach is the FIA model, where a separate organizational structure is created for all aspects of the monitoring program. The separate structure could exist as part of NFS, as part of R&D, or through an outsourcing contract at the national, Regional, or multi-Forest level. Under this model, this separate entity provides the structure for data quality control and carries out all aspects of the monitoring program, from data collection through report preparation. The information is made regularly available to all benefiting Regions and National Forests, for use in relevant planning documents.

The timber cruising model places more burdens on Regional and National Forest programs to provide the personnel for carrying out the program. At the same time, it gives the Regional office and National Forests more control over sample design and any alterations in data collection that might be needed during the course of the program. Maintaining high and consistent levels of effort and quality across multiple administrative structures and years is a critical issue under this model.

The FIA model relieves Regional offices and National Forests from all aspects of monitoring while providing the National Forests with high-quality, scientifically independent information for land management planning purposes. Under this model, a completely separate, dedicated organization is created and relies on special funds. Because the organization is centralized, crews generally are traveling resulting in additional expense associated with travel. When this model is used for animal monitoring, the timing of surveys is critical and the need to deploy crews for simultaneous surveys across large areas becomes an important consideration. The FIA model provides a very direct way to maintain quality control over time and space. However, this model might give the Regional office and National Forests less control over needed changes in the monitoring program unless the separate entity is directly managed by the Regional office, such as under a Regional contract.

The choice of models needs further consideration, along with other potential strategies. It is likely that different models would fit different situations. Given the permanent staffing associated with the FIA model, this approach would be most appropriate for monitoring programs that are truly intended to be long-term in scope with little variance in data collection methods. In contrast, programs with an intended time frame of 10-20 years might fit better under the "timber cruising" model. For now, we simply raise the awareness of the need to choose a specific strategy in order to ensure that multi-Forest and Regional monitoring programs have sufficient coordination and sufficient controls of data quality.

Partnerships _____

Partnerships are essential to the success of wildlife monitoring programs, especially multi-Forest and Regional programs. Virtually all of the current long-term monitoring programs are built on partnerships that bring funding, technical expertise, and/or political muscle to the programs. The Forest Service must not only maintain these partnerships but actively create new partnerships in support of future monitoring programs.

The success of FIA is due in large part to support from external partners, primarily the National Association of State Foresters, the American Forest and Paper Association, the National Council for Air and Stream Improvement, and the Society of American Foresters. These external groups have been effective advocates with Congressional appropriation staffs. Moreover, FIA receives approximately $5,000,000 in partner contributions annually.

Wildlife staffs have an excellent history of building partnerships at national, Regional, and Forest levels for wildlife habitat restoration and enhancement projects, but there are fewer examples of partnerships explicitly created for wildlife monitoring. Some current and potential partnership opportunities are given here.

International Association of Fish and Wildlife Agencies (IAFWA)

IAFWA has been a significant partner with the Forest Service in the realm of habitat restoration and species conservation. IAFWA is in a position to garner support for broad scale monitoring programs, in the same way that state forestry programs influence the funding of the FIA program. In order to get IAFWA's support, however, the Forest Service needs to demonstrate more than a potpourri of local monitoring efforts. IAFWA needs to see a well-planned monitoring design with broad applicability, that supports the states' need for wildlife information, and is practical, scientifically sound, and field tested.

State agencies

Individual state game and fish agencies will continue to be valuable partners in monitoring programs. The success of several landbird monitoring programs, most notably Monitoring Colorado Birds, Songbird Monitoring in the Great Lakes Region, and Nevada Bird Count, are due to strong partnerships with state agencies (Colorado Division of Wildlife, Minnesota Department of Natural Resources, and Nevada Department of Wildlife). The main contribution by state agencies is funding, and states also provide expertise and protocols for data collection. Most states tend to be interested in broad scale monitoring designs that can be implemented statewide. Whereas IAFWA can provide the leverage for federal funding across all states, individual state agencies provide the local contacts for developing joint monitoring programs at Regional and multi-Forest levels. The funding for individual states will likely be from the State Wildlife Grants program.

BLM, NPS, DOD, and Tribes

Tribal agencies and federal land management agencies are crucial partners for context and targeted monitoring programs. All broad scale monitoring efforts will require partnerships with multiple landowners in order to provide a more complete and integrated monitoring effort. In addition to providing a more complete sampling frame, land management agencies can provide financial support to mutually fund a person or entity (or university) to coordinate data collection and management.

USGS

Partnership opportunities with USGS are currently underutilized. USGS brings expertise in ecological classification and mapping, access to the largest landbird monitoring database, the Breeding Bird Survey data, and access to statistical expertise and data analysis tools. Opportunities for partnerships exist with the Patuxent Research Station, with the USGS Status and Trends of Biological Resources program, and with individual USGS coop units.

NatureServe

The Forest Service has an MOU with NatureServe that addresses shared goals of inventory and assessments, ecological classification and mapping, data sharing, and technology development. NatureServe's expansive database, along with habitat classification and mapping capabilities, makes it an ideal partner for context monitoring. Currently, the Forest Service NRIS database works best at the National Forest scale, but data sharing with NatureServe could boost NRIS capability to display and evaluate data at multi-Forest and Regional scales. A key Forest Service contact in this partnership would be the FAUNA development team.

Other NGOs

The Forest Service has many successful partnerships with organizations that support conservation of game birds and mammals (e.g., Rocky Mountain Elk Foundation, National Wild Turkey Federation, Northern Wild Sheep and Goat Council). Although the focus of these partnerships is habitat restoration, the organizations also support monitoring programs for the targeted species. The National Wildlife Federation and Defenders of Wildlife are partners to a number of monitoring programs for federally listed species. Other potential partners include the National Audubon Society, Partners in Amphibian and Reptile Conservation, and various state-based conservation organizations.

Volunteers

There is significant opportunity to use volunteers to assist with collection of monitoring data. When a monitoring program has a clearly established sample design and field protocol, an effective data quality assurance component, and adequate training and supervision, the contributions of volunteers can be substantial. The Student Conservation Association provides college students with conservation internships while providing agencies with volunteers for the cost of per diem, and these volunteers have been used in thousands of state and federal projects across the country. The Citizen Science Program is a successful partnership between Cornell University and various agencies, using volunteers for data collection. The Forest Service was a recent partner in a Citizens Science Program project that looked at the effects of recreation on a suite of nesting forest birds. Cornell University took the lead with sample design development, volunteer training, and data analysis.

32

USDA Forest Service Gen. Tech. Rep. RMRS-GTR-161. 2005

Chapter 7

Critical Elements for Successful Monitoring

Current monitoring programs for terrestrial wildlife and habitats do not provide all the information necessary for adaptive management. Inadequacies in monitoring programs are long-standing, not restricted to the Forest Service, and difficult to resolve. In a 1993 report commissioned by then-Chief of the Forest Service Dale Robertson (U.S. Forest Service 1993), the following problems with monitoring programs were noted:

- Monitoring and evaluation is viewed as another "new" program which will require more money, more time, and more people-resources which are already stressed.
- Monitoring and evaluation requirements often are not based on clear objectives, do not address key management questions or do not address key issues.
- There is no incentive for doing monitoring and evaluation, and little or no perceived risk for not doing it.
- Monitoring and evaluation is not recognized as an integral part of target accomplishment.
- Monitoring and evaluation costs increase unit-costs which can adversely affect budget allocations.
- There is a lack of integration and interdisciplinary approach in monitoring and evaluation activities resulting in duplication of efforts and redundant or inconsistent data.
- Monitoring and evaluation techniques, methodologies, and philosophies vary widely resulting in inconsistent findings and reporting methods that affect our credibility.
- Effective teamwork within the Forest Service and with other agencies, partners and public is not readily apparent.
- Appropriate scientific methods frequently are not used in conducting monitoring and evaluation.

While some progress has been made, it is telling that many of the same concerns apply to today's monitoring programs. Monitoring is a complex issue that requires the allocation of significant resources. There are clearly no rapid or easy paths to effective monitoring, and it takes a major commitment to improve monitoring. The following are key recommendations for continuing improvement of monitoring of terrestrial animals and their habitats:

- Make a national commitment to improve monitoring of terrestrial animals and their habitats.
- Ensure that all monitoring contributes to adaptive management by exploring both the causes for trends and alternative scenarios that could reverse unfavorable trends.
- Ensure that all monitoring complies with USDA Data Quality Guidelines.
- Implement Regional monitoring strategies that integrate habitat and population monitoring. Monitoring habitat alone will rarely be sufficient for adaptive management because habitat relationships are not well understood and may not be predictable.
- Adopt and integrate three types of monitoring (context, targeted, and cause-and-effect).
- Use sound ecological principles and risk assessment to prioritize and design monitoring activities.
- Recognize that monitoring is multi-scalar. Coordinate across ecological and administrative scales, with emphasis on the role of the Regions.
- Establish appropriate roles and coordination for NFS and R&D from WO through Forest levels.
- Provide adequate staffing, skills, and funding structures to accomplish monitoring objectives.
- Use partnerships and interagency coordination to accomplish monitoring objectives.
- Ensure that individuals and teams responsible for monitoring, development, and oversight have appropriate skills.

Following these recommendations would allow the Forest Service, in conjunction with partners and collaborators, to identify appropriate monitoring questions and designs for terrestrial animals and habitats and collect data needed for adaptive management over the long-term.

Literature Cited _____

Andelman, S., J. S. Beissinger, J. Cochrane, L. Gerber, P. Gomez-Priego, C. Groves, J. Haufler, R. Holthausen, D. Lee, L. Maguire, B. Noon, K. Ralls, and H. Regan. 2001. Scientific standards for conducting viability assessments under the National Forest

USDA Forest Service Gen. Tech. Rep. RMRS-GTR-161. 2005

33

Management Act: Report and recommendations of the NCEAS working group. National Center for Ecological Analysis and Synthesis, University of California, Santa Barbara, CA.

Barnes, R. B. 1979. Wildlife habitat from a forest resource inventory: is it possible? Transactions of the Northeast Section of the Wildlife Society 36:151-159.

Beissinger, S.R. and D.R. McCullough. 2002. Population viability analysis. University of Chicago Press. Chicago, IL.

Brooks, R. T. 1990. Status and trends of raptor habitat in the northeast. Pages 123-132 in B. G. Pendleton, editor. Proceedings of the northeast raptor management symposium and workshop. Institute for Wildlife Research, National Wildlife Federation, Scientific and Technical Series No. 13. Washington, DC.

Brooks, R. T., S. Frieswyk, and A. Ritter. 1986. Forest wildlife habitat statistics for Maine 1982. USDA Forest Service Northeastern Station, Resource Bulletin NE-96, Amherst, MA.

Caughley, G. 1977. Analysis of vertebrate populations. John Wiley and Sons, New York, N.Y. 234 pp.

Chojnacky, D. C. and J. L. Dick. 2000. Evaluating FIA forest inventory data for monitoring Mexican spotted owl habitat: Gila National Forest example. Western Journal of Applied Forestry 15(4):195-199.

Ellingson, A. R. and P. M. Lukacs. 2003. Improving methods for regional landbird monitoring: a reply to Hutto and Young. Wildlife Society Bulletin 31:896-902.

Flather, C. H., T. W. Hoekstra, D. E. Chalk, N. D. Cost, and V. A. Rudis. 1989. Recent historical and projected Regional trends of white-tailed deer and wild turkey in the southern United States. USDA Forest Service General Technical Report RM-172. Fort Collins, CO.

Franklin, A. B., R. J. Gutiérrez, J. D. Nichols, M. R. Seamans, G. C. White, G. S. Zimmerman, J. E. Hines, T. E. Munton, W. S. LaHaye, J. A. Blakesley, G. N Steger, B. R. Noon, S. W. H. Shaw, J. J. Keane, T. L. McDonald, and S. Britting. 2004. Population dynamics of the California Spotted Owl (*Strix occidentalis occidentalis*): a meta-analysis. Ornithological Monographs No. 54, The American Ornithologists' Union, Washington, DC.

Hutto, R. L., and J. S. Young. 2002. Use of a landbird monitoring database to explore effects of partial-cut timber harvesting. Forest Science 48:373-378.

Hutto, R. L. and J. S. Young. 2003. On the design of monitoring programs and the use of population indices: a reply to Ellingson and Lukacs. Wildlife Society Bulletin 31:903-910.

Kareiva, P. and U. Wennergren. 1995. Connecting landscape patterns to ecosystem and population processes. Nature 373:299-302.

Karr, J. R. and D. R. Dudley. 1981. Ecological perspective on water quality goals. Environmental Management 5:55-68.

Lebreton, J.-D., K. P. Burnham, J. Clobert, D. R. Anderson. 1992. Modelling survival and testing biological hypotheses using marked animals: a unified approach with case studies. Ecological Monographs 62:67-118.

Lee, K. N. 1993. Compass and gyroscope: integrating science and politics for the environment. Island Press, Washington, DC.

MacKenzie, D. I., J. D. Nichols, G. B. Lachman, S. Droege, J. A. Royle, and C. A. Langtimm. 2002. Estimating site occupancy rates when detection probabilities are less than one. Ecology 83:2248-2255.

Manley, P. N., W. J. Zielinski, M. D. Schleisinger, and S. R. Mori. 2004. Evaluation of a multiple-species approach to monitoring species at the ecoregional scale. Ecological Applications 14(1):296-310.

Maurer, B. A. 1994. Geographical population analysis: tools for the analysis of biodiversity. Blackwell Scientific Publications, Boston, MD.

McKelvey, K. S. and D. E. Pearson, 2001. Population estimation with sparse data: the role of estimators versus indices revisited. Canadian Journal of Zoology 79(10):1754-1765.

O'Brien, R. A. 1990. Assessment of nongame bird habitat using forest survey data. USDA Forest Service Intermountain Research Station Research Paper INT-431. Ogden, UT.

Ohmann, J. L., W. C. McComb, and A. A. Zumrawi. 1994. Snag abundance for primary cavity-nesting birds on nonfederal forest lands in Oregon and Washington. Wildlife Society Bulletin 22:607-620.

Otis, D. L., K. P. Burnham, G. C. White, and D. R. Anderson. 1978. Statistical inference from capture data on closed animal populations. Wildlife Monographs 62.

Pimm, S. L. 1991. The balance of nature? Ecological issues in the conservation of species and communities. University of Chicago Press, Chicago, IL.

Pollock, K. H., J. D. Nichols, C. Brownie, and J. E. Hines. 1990. Statistical inference for capture-recapture experiments. Wildlife Monographs 107.

Raphael, M. G., R. G. Anthony, S. DeStefano, E. D. Forsman, A. B. Franklin, R. Holthausen, E. C. Meslow, and B. R. Noon. 1996. Use, interpretation, and implications of demographic analyses of northern spotted owl populations. Studies in Avian Biology 17:102-112.

Royle, J. A., and J. D. Nichols. 2003. Estimating abundance from repeated presence-absence data or point counts. Ecology 84:777-790.

Rudis, Victor A. 2004. *Quarter Century of Multipurpose Forest Inventories in the United States.* http://www.msstate.edu/dept/forestry/biblio.html.

Tilman, D., R. M. May, C. L. Lehman, and M. A. Nowak. 1994. Habitat destruction and the extinction debt. Nature 371:65-66.

Tyre, A. J., B. Tenhumberg, S. A. Field, D. Niejalke, K. Parris, and H. P. Possingham. 2003. Improving precision and reducing bias in biological surveys: estimating false-negative error rates. Ecological Applications 13:1790-1801.

Walters, C. and C. S. Holling. 1990. Large-scale management experiments and learning by doing. Ecology 71:2060-2068.

USDA Forest Service. 1993. National Monitoring and Evaluation Strategy. United States Department of Agriculture, Forest Service. Washington Office. Washington, DC.

Young, J. S., and R. L. Hutto. 1999. Habitat and landscape factors affecting cowbird distribution in the Northern Rockies. Studies in Avian Biology 18:41-51.

34

USDA Forest Service Gen. Tech. Rep. RMRS-GTR-161. 2005

RMRS
ROCKY MOUNTAIN RESEARCH STATION

The Rocky Mountain Research Station develops scientific information and technology to improve management, protection, and use of the forests and rangelands. Research is designed to meet the needs of National Forest managers, Federal and State agencies, public and private organizations, academic institutions, industry, and individuals.

Studies accelerate solutions to problems involving ecosystems, range, forests, water, recreation, fire, resource inventory, land reclamation, community sustainability, forest engineering technology, multiple use economics, wildlife and fish habitat, and forest insects and diseases. Studies are conducted cooperatively, and applications may be found worldwide.

Research Locations

Flagstaff, Arizona
Fort Collins, Colorado*
Boise, Idaho
Moscow, Idaho
Bozeman, Montana
Missoula, Montana

Reno, Nevada
Albuquerque, New Mexico
Rapid City, South Dakota
Logan, Utah
Ogden, Utah
Provo, Utah

*Station Headquarters, Natural Resources Research Center, 2150 Centre Avenue, Building A, Fort Collins, CO 80526

www.ingramcontent.com/pod-product-compliance
Lightning Source LLC
Chambersburg PA
CBHW080627290526
45790CB00007B/2961